Sunset

GARDEN DESIGNS

BY PHILIP EDINGER AND THE EDITORS OF SUNSET BOOKS

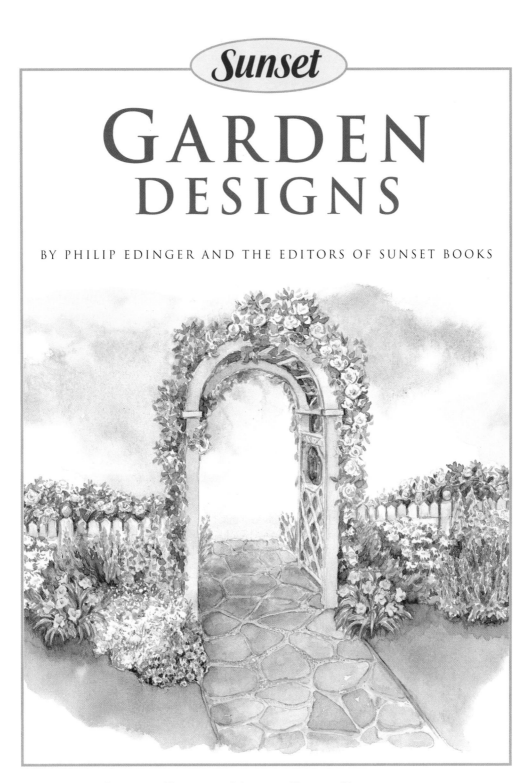

SUNSET BOOKS · MENLO PARK, CALIFORNIA

PLOTS AND PLANS

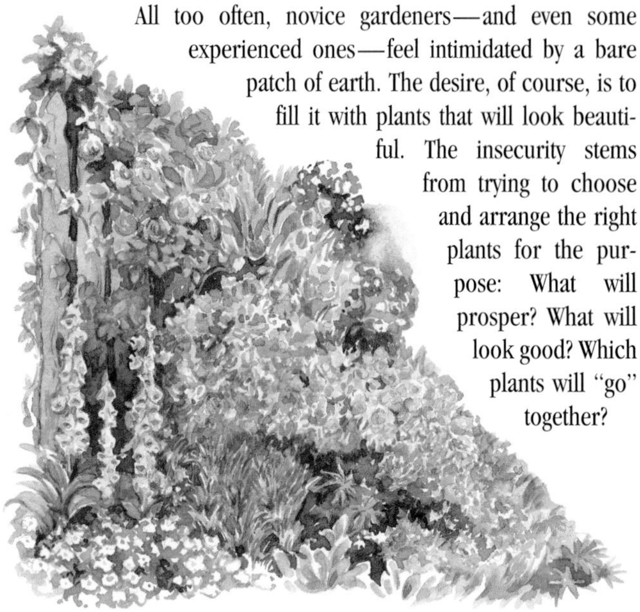

All too often, novice gardeners—and even some experienced ones—feel intimidated by a bare patch of earth. The desire, of course, is to fill it with plants that will look beautiful. The insecurity stems from trying to choose and arrange the right plants for the purpose: What will prosper? What will look good? Which plants will "go" together?

In this book, you'll find answers to those questions. Beginning on page 12 is a series of 88 plans—some addressing the typical garden situations that confront home gardeners everywhere, others offering ideas for the kinds of special plantings many gardeners long to have. For the most part, these designs will occupy only part of your landscape; those dealing with the total garden area are small plans for postage-stamp yards.

The choice of designs presented here is wide enough to suit almost any situation and any climate. You'll find plantings for Northeast or Southwest, sun or shade, lawn or paved patio, public areas or plots sequestered for private enjoyment. You may, indeed, discover a plan that fits your needs exactly. Part of the beauty of these designs, however, lies in their ability to inspire. As you study the plant combinations presented in each one, you'll absorb the basic design principles reviewed on pages 6–9 and gain the confidence to devise successful plans of your own.

Proceed with pencil in one hand, shovel in the other!

SUNSET BOOKS

Vice President and General Manager: Richard A. Smeby
Vice President , Editorial Director: Bob Doyle
Production Director: Lory Day
Art Director: Vasken Guiragossian

Staff for this book:

Managing Editor: Joan Beth Erickson
Sunset Books Senior Editor, Gardening: Suzanne Normand Eyre
Copy Editor and Indexer: Rebecca LaBrum
Photo Researcher: Tishana Peebles
Production Coordinator: Patricia S. Williams
Special Contributors: Bridget Biscotti Bradley, Barbara Brown, Sally Lauten, Jean Warboy

Art Director: Alice Rogers
Computer Production: Linda Bouchard, Joan Olson
Map Design and Cartography: Reineck & Reineck, San Francisco

10 9 8 7 6

First printing January 2000
For additional copies of *Garden Designs* or any other *Sunset* book, call 1-800-526-5111 or visit us at *www.sunsetbooks.com*

GARDEN DESIGNERS:

Philip Edinger for all illustrated gardens except the following: **Kathleen Norris Brenzel:** 82; **Gary Patterson:** 44, 63, 86; **Truxell & Valentino Landscape Development:** 24.

ILLUSTRATORS:

Gwendolyn Babbitt: 34, 35, 66–67, 74–75, 94, 95, 96, 97; **Marcie Hawthorne:** 12 top, 16, 17, 36, 37, 76, 77, 92, 93; **Lois Lovejoy:** 18, 19, 22, 23, 39, 42, 43, 44, 46, 47, 63, 64, 65, 68, 82, 83, 84, 85, 86, 87; **Mimi Osborne:** 12 bottom left; **Erin O'Toole:** 1, 2, 8, 10, 14, 15, 24, 25, 26, 27, 28, 29, 32, 33, 38, 40, 41, 48, 49, 50, 51, 52, 53, 54, 55, 56, 57, 58, 62, 69, 70, 71, 72, 73, 78, 79, 80, 81, 90, 91, 98, 99, 100, 101, 102, 103, 104, 105, back cover top right, bottom left; **Lucy Sargeant:** 7 bottom; **Elayne Sears:** 13, 20, 21, 30, 31, 45, 60, 61, 88–89, back cover top left; **Jenny Speckels:** all plot plan illustrations.

PHOTOGRAPHERS:

Dariel Alexander: 3 bottom, 58; **Marion Brenner:** 30, 33; **Gay Bumgarner:** 88 bottom; **David Cavagnaro:** 57 bottom, 67 bottom, 70, 74, 80, 82; **Claire Curran:** 29 bottom; **Daybreak Imagery, Richard Day:** 88 top; **Derek Fell:** 9 top; **Philip Harvey:** 9 bottom; **Saxon Holt:** 6, 7 top, 31, 56, 83, 104; **Allan Mandell:** 3 top, 4; **Charles Mann:** 16 top, 29 top, 43, 57 top, 62, 86; **Jerry Pavia:** 46, 88 center; **Joanne Pavia:** 36, 67 center; **Norman A. Plate:** 50; **Lauren Springer:** 3 center, 10; **Michael S. Thompson:** 32, 34, 40, 41, 95; **Wayside Gardens:** 16 bottom; **Doug Wilson:** 24; **Cynthia Woodyard:** 18, 42, 63; **Tom Wyatt:** 67 top.

Cover: This pocket-size garden features an harmonious mix of delphinium, meadow sweet, catmint, foxglove, dianthus, 'Silver Brocade' beach wormwood, and thyme. Garden design by Teena Garay. Cover design by Vasken Guiragossian. Photography by Norman A. Plate. Border photo by Connie Coleman.

CONTENTS

Why do some gardens "work," while others simply look jumbled, boring, or undistinguished? The answer is "advance planning"—but that can be hard to believe, since so many appealing gardens have a natural look that seems to deny the existence of an underlying plan.

GARDENING BY
DESIGN

In this book, you'll discover that planning is indeed the secret of a successful garden, but that not all plans are obvious or rigid. You'll also come to realize that advance planning doesn't have to dictate hours at the drawing board with T square and triangle. Some of our designs are precisely laid out, but others are unabashedly free-form. Some deal with total outdoor space where that space is small, but most illustrate planting schemes that fit within a larger garden framework, addressing typical landscape problems and situations—and garden wish lists, too.

Regardless of size or style, all our plans aim to show you how to develop pleasing designs through effective plant combination. And all are adaptable, too. You can use them as blueprints or as points of departure: replicate them exactly for guaranteed enjoyable plantings and gardens, or just let them suggest lovely combinations you can adjust to your particular needs.

Foliage in a range of sizes, shapes, textures, and colors brings three-season interest to this lightly shaded garden. Design by Dan Heims.

A robust planting of favorite perennials forms a multicolored mosaic of flowers and leaves in a sunny entry garden.

WHAT DO YOU WANT?

No two homes present exactly the same garden-design challenges, and not all gardeners see the same solution to similar problems. Thus, no two gardens are alike, not even if one was originally intended to be an exact replica of the other.

With this firmly in mind, we have assembled 88 attractive and imaginative plans to address familiar garden situations, typical problems, and popular gardening themes (seasonal color, rose gardens, and many more). Many designs suit a wide range of climate zones; others focus on particular regions with special gardening advantages or limitations. To learn where your area fits into *Sunset*'s climate zone scheme, see pages 106–109.

The plans are divided into two groups. The first covers common garden situations, while the second involves plantings with a theme or a special purpose.

COMMON GARDEN SITUATIONS

On pages 12–57, you'll find plans designed to handle landscaping challenges common to virtually all homes. "First Impressions" (pages 12–27) tackles the transition area between sidewalk and front door, a space often overlooked as a potential beauty spot. "Filling in the Blanks" (pages 28–43) shows a variety of ways to approach planting along fences and house walls, in shady patches and hot spots, and in open expanses of lawn or bare ground. "Thinking Small" (pages 44–57) offers beautiful gardens just right for the ever-shrinking suburban yard (including those yards that are entirely deck or patio) and also covers two traditional limited-space problem spots—narrow side yards and parking strips.

SPECIALTY PLANTINGS

In this collection are designs for gardens with a theme or a purpose—herb plots, cut-flower gardens, lovely shrub borders, and numerous others. Many of these fit neatly into a larger framework: you can install an herb nook near the back door, for example, and still have plenty of garden left to devote to another design (or designs).

"Themes and Variations" (pages 60–77) presents plans highlighting seasonal flowers, schemes for cottage-style gardens and rose gardens, and plantings to enhance a backyard pool or pond. The gardens in "Designed for a Purpose" (pages 78–93) have a theme, too, but it's one with a functional element: these plans provide more than beauty. Some give flowers for cutting, others attract birds and butterflies; you'll also find plantings supplying scented flowers and foliage, five herb gardens, and a traditional kitchen garden. "Color Gardens" (pages 94–105) focuses strictly on color and color combinations. Look here for hot-color, cool-color, mixed-color, and all-white plantings; gardens of gray or silver foliage with white or pastel blossoms; and plantings in which foliage provides almost all the color.

COMBINING PLANTS EFFECTIVELY

Cottage gardens (see pages 66–68) seem to prove that planting without a plan can succeed brilliantly: they look casual, almost haphazard, their beauty derived from almost limitless variety. We now realize, however, that many of the original cottagers' apparently random plans were governed by an innate sense of design. In modern parlance, this design sense is known as *effective plant combination.*

Though they address myriad specific situations, the plans presented on pages 12–105 all rely on effective plant combination. All follow the same basic tenets, making each plant choice on the basis of color, texture, shape, and size. We review these basics below; you'll find them invaluable guidelines when you adapt or modify plans.

Contrast lends vitality to a planting. Here, foliage and blossoms offer equal interest.

COLOR

For most of us, the word "garden" is virtually synonymous with "color" (vegetable gardens excepted, of course!). Visit any garden center or plant outlet, and you're tempted by ranks of colorful flowers ready for spur-of-the-moment purchase and immediate planting. But not all colors assort well or compete equally, and the planting assembled on impulse may end up the floral equivalent of an out-of-tune brass choir.

The subject of color is complex enough to warrant entire books of its own (see, for example, *Sunset*'s *Gardening with Color*). Nonetheless, it's possible to make a few simple, general statements.

Light colors advance, dark ones retreat. Warm colors usually combine well with warm colors, cool ones with other cool colors and white. Pastel shades generally look good together but may lack "punch." Combined bright colors, on the other hand, can pack too much punch—they can be attractive in combination, but their tendency to vie with each other for attention can give a planting a rather strident look. In bright-plus-pastel plantings, the brights tend to dominate, even if they're in the minority.

In combining dissimilar colors, you can achieve good contrasts with primary colors (yellow, red, blue) and with complementary colors

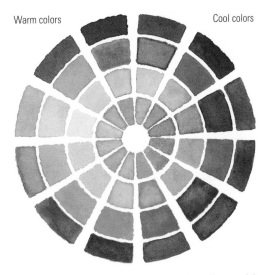

Warm colors   Cool colors

The primary colors (red, blue, yellow) are spaced equally around the color wheel; transitional colors connect them. Warm colors appear on the left side of the wheel, cool colors on the right.

(those opposite each other on the color wheel) such as blue and orange or yellow and violet.

Size matters. A soft yellow hollyhock can command more attention than a brilliant gold French marigold simply because there is more of it to draw the eye.

Petal texture or sheen also affects a color's projection: a shiny-petaled red flower, for example, will stand out more than one of the same shade with matte, nonreflective petals.

TEXTURE

Whether you're working with flowers or focusing on foliage, texture is probably the most frequently overlooked design element. In simple terms, textural contrast arises from mixing various sizes (large to small) and different shapes (broad to narrow).

Sometimes you can achieve a stunning textural mix by using variations of just one plant. Hosta cultivars, for example, include plants with great paddlelike leaves as well as those with tiny spoonlike or dagger-shaped foliage, and there are countless leaf sizes and shapes in between. More often, though, textural interest derives from joining radically different plants: think, for example, of filmy common yarrow in combination with fountainlike eulalia grass and the broad, sandpapery leaves of purple coneflower.

Among flowers alone, the variations are seemingly limitless. Just consider the tiny blossoms of baby's breath, borne in airy sprays; lush, large, many-petaled roses; daisylike flowers, from simple asters to mammoth dahlias; the bell-shaped blossoms of the various campanulas; and the chalicelike blooms of daylilies. Manner of floral presentation offers yet another textural variation. Spikes of flowers—as in delphinium, hollyhock, and snapdragon—can provide vertical contrast to the flattened heads of yarrow or sedum blossoms or the starburst drumsticks of lily-of-the-nile and ornamental allium.

READING THE PLANS

For each design in this book, a watercolor illustration depicts the planting in its peak season. Accompanying the illustration is a plot plan that shows the entire planted area. Within the plan, the area occupied by each kind of plant is shaded in the basic color of its foliage or flowers and labeled with a letter. These letters correspond to those in the accompanying plant list, where the plants used are listed by botanical name and common name (if there is one). The total number of each plant needed for the plan is indicated in parentheses (for certain ground-cover plants typically sold by the flat, we do not give a number, but simply indicate the appropriate plant spacing). To see where a plant fits into the design, check for its letter on the plan.

The example below (taken from page 29) shows how to read the plans on pages 12–105.

PLAN ILLUSTRATION
AND DESCRIPTION

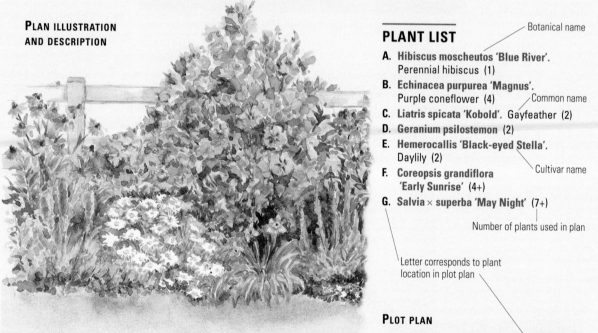

BEAUTIFUL BOUNDARY

Some fences are quite open in structure, marking boundaries without creating visual barriers—as here, where a post-and-rail fence defines the edge of a cultivated garden while allowing a clear view into the wild meadow beyond. Given regular moisture and a full-sun location, this varied floral assortment delivers a summer's worth of color. The plants are all herbaceous perennials, dying back to the ground or to low tufts of foliage when the growing season ends. A quick cleanup in late winter readies the planting for spring growth. This plan is especially well suited to Zones 32–41 but will also succeed in Zones 2–9, 14–21.

Botanical name

PLANT LIST

A. **Hibiscus moscheutos 'Blue River'.** Perennial hibiscus (1)

B. **Echinacea purpurea 'Magnus'.** Purple coneflower (4) — Common name

C. **Liatris spicata 'Kobold'.** Gayfeather (2)

D. **Geranium psilostemon** (2)

E. **Hemerocallis 'Black-eyed Stella'.** Daylily (2)

Cultivar name

F. **Coreopsis grandiflora 'Early Sunrise'** (4+)

G. **Salvia × superba 'May Night'** (7+)

Number of plants used in plan

Letter corresponds to plant location in plot plan

PLOT PLAN

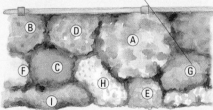

Planting area: 22' x 6'

Dimensions of planting

Climate zones suitable for planting (see pages 106–109)

SHAPE

One reason a planting of just one kind of flower often looks monotonous is that all the plants are built alike. There's no variation in overall appearance. The most interesting gardens assort plants of varied outlines: upright, rounded, spreading, fountainlike, and so forth. Factor texture into this equation, and the combinations are virtually endless. Upright shapes alone, for example, include all sorts of outlines, from the spirelike blossom stems of hollyhock and mullein to swordlike iris foliage and pencil-like conifers to bushy but upward-thrusting lupine. Some spreading plants, such as lamb's ears, are essentially low growing but produce upright flower stems at bloom time.

SIZE AND DENSITY

The time-honored rule of "tall in back, short in front" is still good advice: you wouldn't plant a husky viburnum at the front of a bed and diminutive forget-me-nots behind it. Still, the rule does allow exceptions for the sake of contrast. You can effectively accent some taller and/or bulkier plants by giving them a more forward position and surrounding them with shorter plants that provide a setting. In such cases, density also can come into play. A larger plant with some see-through quality—witch hazel and some kinds of mahonias, for example—can be showcased closer to the front of a border. Consider size and texture together, too; you'll find that a bulky, small-leafed plant at the rear of a planting will seem to be located farther back than will a bulky plant with large leaves.

PUTTING THE PLANTS IN PLACE

For the most part, the plants called for in these plans are not unusual or hard to find. Many are sold in local nurseries, garden centers, and even in the garden departments of hardware and home-improvement emporia. Established mail-order nurseries likewise stock most of these plants, and they often carry numerous less-common types as well.

Timing is important when setting out plants. As a general rule of thumb, plant when roots can begin growing in cool, moist soil and when new growth can unfold in cool to mild weather. Given these conditions, plants establish more rapidly and perform better in their first season.

Where winters are fairly mild (Zones 4–9, 12–31), trees, shrubs, and most perennials are best planted from midautumn through winter; where summers are cool, planting time can extend into spring. In colder regions (Zones 1–3, 10, 11, 32–45), most plants are best set out in late winter or early spring, though fall planting is also possible if the plants are given winter freeze protection.

Mail-order nurseries try to ship each plant at the preferred planting time; retail nurseries are usually well stocked at optimum planting times.

Varied shapes, textures, and colors combine in a garden that highlights the individual beauty of each plant, yet presents an harmonious overall picture.

Container-grown plants are available everywhere for planting throughout the growing season, and it's hard to resist the odd impulse purchase in spring and summer. Be aware, though, that plants set out during the warmer months will need close attention to watering and may require some shelter from wind and sun. Their relatively small, unestablished root systems are more subject to drying than are roots of established plants and may have trouble drawing enough moisture from the soil to replace that lost through transpiration in hot, windy weather.

For details on soils, planting techniques, and general care, consult Sunset's *Basic Gardening Illustrated*.

Plotting a planting bed is easier if you outline the bed (and even the planting areas within it) in powdered chalk, flour, or a common soil amendment such as gypsum or lime.

COMMON GARDEN

SITUATIONS

Old or new, cutting-edge contemporary or frankly old-fashioned, brick or clapboard, grand or modest—there's no counting the ways in which one house can differ from another. Still, despite their endless variety, all houses share certain outdoor features that often present challenges for garden design. In this chapter, we offer solutions for many such situations.

We lead off with the approach to the front door: the transition from public to private domain. Suggestions range from dressing up a walkway with beds or borders to converting the entire front yard to garden. Next, we turn to ideas for coping with blank spots: fences and house walls, completely shaded areas beneath trees, unrelieved stretches of lawn or even gravel that cry out for the adornment of a colorful "island."

Creating beauty in limited spaces is a challenge most gardeners face at one time or another. If you have a small backyard, you can turn the whole space into a garden, perhaps keeping just a postage-stamp plot of lawn. If your back (or front!) yard is nothing more than a deck or patio, don't despair—four plans will help you turn these areas from stark to stunning. You'll also find dazzling designs for two familiar problem spots: narrow side yards and parking strips.

A densely planted bed of roses and durable spring- and summer-blooming perennials fills a long, narrow space between sidewalk and fence. Design by Lauren Springer.

FIRST IMPRESSIONS

The short trip from public space to private front door offers guests their first glimpse of your domain. At its most basic, the path is an unadorned concrete ribbon that takes dead aim from sidewalk to door, bisecting a lawn on the way—or, where there's an attached garage, making a dogleg progression from driveway to entrance. Such bald pedestrian efficiency is neither inspiring to your guests nor uplifting for you—so why not chart a more imaginative course? The designs on these 16 pages present a variety of appealing entry plantings; all can be adapted to existing situations or created from scratch if you're remodeling a landscape or starting on a new home.

FORMAL ENTRY IN TWO STYLES

The arrow-straight entry walk is inherently formal—a characteristic you can choose to accentuate or to soften. The treatments shown here illustrate both approaches, with the striking difference in appearance achieved strictly through choice of plants.

The rigidly formal scheme at lower left (Style A) gains its effect from manicured plants in an obviously symmetrical arrangement. This simple design can succeed in Zones 3–9, 14–24, 32–34 (warmest part). The plan shown above (Style B) has the same regular plant placement and repetition as the first, but soft contours and fluffy, irregular edges lend it an almost informal feeling. These plants will grow in mild-winter climate Zones 8, 9, 12–28.

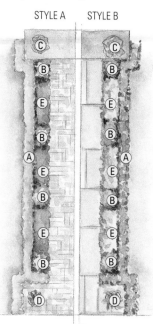

Entry walk: 27' long

PLANT LIST
STYLE A

A. **Buxus microphylla japonica 'Green Beauty'.** Japanese boxwood (44)
B. **Platycladus orientalis 'Bonita'.** Oriental arborvitae (8)
C. **Taxus baccata 'Stricta'.** Irish yew (2)
D. **Liriope muscari 'Silvery Sunproof'.** Big blue lily turf (2)
E. **Vinca minor 'Ralph Shugert'.** Dwarf periwinkle (18)

PLANT LIST
STYLE B

A. **Lavandula angustifolia 'Hidcote' or 'Twickel Purple'.** English lavender (44)
B. **Punica granatum 'Chico'.** Dwarf pomegranate (8)
C. **Nerium oleander 'Petite Salmon'.** Oleander (2)
D. **Phormium 'Bronze Baby'.** New Zealand flax (2)
E. **Gazania hybrids in pink, salmon, cream, white (18)**

CURVED WALK WITH FREE-FORM PLANTING

Surprising though it may seem, the natural walking path between two unobstructed points is not a straight line but a gently sinuous curve. Establishing such a route from sidewalk to front door gives the approach the feel of a relaxed amble rather than a no-time-to-spare rush—and offers ample opportunity for plantings that will delight even the casual passerby.

The plant assortment shown here features color from both blossoms and foliage, providing interest over at least three seasons. The plan works best where it gets just a touch of shade (as from high, open trees) during the afternoon. It's most successful in Zones 4–6, 32, 34, 37, and 39, but you can also enjoy it in Zones 3, 35, 36, 38, 40, and 41 by using *Rhododendron* (azalea) 'Orchid Lights' in place of *R. mucronulatum* 'Cornell Pink' (B in the list below) and replacing *R.* 'Boule de Neige' (C) with *Hydrangea arborescens* 'Annabelle'.

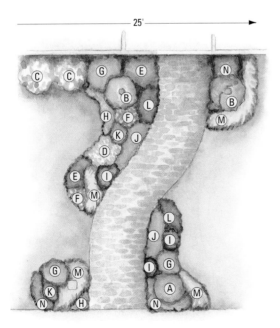

PLANT LIST

A. Acer palmatum 'Ornatum'.
   Red laceleaf Japanese maple (1)

B. Rhododendron mucronulatum
   'Cornell Pink' (2)

C. Rhododendron 'Boule de Neige' (2+)

D. Daphne × burkwoodii 'Carol Mackie' (1)

E. Helleborus niger. Christmas rose (6)

F. Astrantia major. Masterwort (3)

G. Alchemilla mollis. Lady's-mantle (7)

H. Heuchera 'Palace Purple' (7)

I. Bergenia 'Bressingham Ruby' (5)

J. Astilbe simplicifolia 'Sprite' (9)

K. Hosta 'Krossa Regal' (2)

L. Hosta tardiflora (9)

M. Hakonechloa macra 'Aureola'.
   Japanese forest grass (16)

N. Ajuga reptans. Carpet bugle (18+)

PLANT LIST

A. **Hamamelis × intermedia 'Ruby Glow'.**
Witch hazel (1)

B. **Magnolia 'Betty'** (1)

C. **Enkianthus campanulatus** (1)

D. **Pinus mugo mugo.** Mugho pine (1)

E. **Rhododendron yakushimanum
'Koichiro Wada'** (2)

F. **Erica darleyensis 'Silberschmelze'.**
Heath (5)

G. **Erica 'Dawn'.** Heath (7)

H. **Calluna vulgaris 'Nana'.**
Heather (6)

I. **Viburnum davidii** (2)

J. **Juniperus conferta.**
Shore juniper (3)

K. **Epimedium × versicolor 'Sulphureum'.**
Bishop's hat (11)

L. **Helleborus orientalis.**
Lenten rose (9)

M. **Heuchera 'Palace Purple'** (16)

N. **Imperata cylindrica 'Red Baron' ('Rubra').**
Japanese blood grass (10)

O. **Campanula portenschlagiana
(C. muralis).** Dalmatian bellflower (9)

P. **Sagina subulata 'Aurea'.**
Scotch moss (eighteen to twenty 3-inch
squares, spaced 6 inches apart)

Q. **Ajuga reptans.** Carpet bugle (15)

R. **Rhododendron (azalea) 'Coral Bells'** (2)

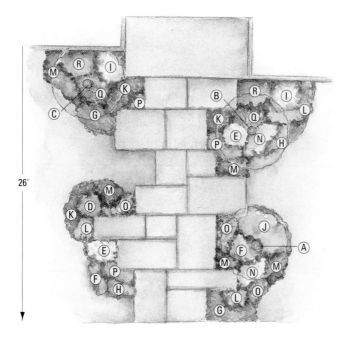

DIVERSIONARY
TACTIC

Deliberate asymmetry disguises the fact that this entry path actually moves directly from sidewalk to front door. Rectangular pavers of different sizes are laid out in a staggered pattern, their edges softened with irregularly shaped planting beds—and the eye sees meandering twists and turns, not a straight line.

Suitable for Pacific Northwest Zones 4–6 and coastal California Zones 15–17, this scheme offers year-round visual interest. There's no mass color display; blossoms on shrubs and perennials come and go from midwinter through fall, while the foliage of various perennials and low shrubs offers more sustained color. In winter, the bare limbs of deciduous shrubs serve as living sculpture.

DIRECT ACCESS

No doubt about it: this path gets you to the front door in a straight line. Yet the walkway is also part of a larger design comprising the three rectangular beds that flank and intersect it.

Suited to mild-winter California and the arid Southwest (Zones 8, 9, 12–24), the planting appears lush, but all its members require just moderate watering. The pebble-aggregate path reflects the stoniness of a natural landscape; Spanish tile insets echo one of the region's favorite architectural inspirations. Floral color is at its height in spring, before the inevitable heat in many of the zones noted above slows or stops growth for the summer.

PLANT LIST

- **A. Phormium 'Maori Chief'.** New Zealand flax (1)
- **B. Cistus 'Doris Hibberson'.** Rockrose (2)
- **C. Cistus 'Warley Rose'.** Rockrose (3)
- **D. Convolvulus cneorum.** Bush morning glory (8)
- **E. Convolvulus mauritanicus.** Ground morning glory (6)
- **F. Euphorbia × martinii** (5)
- **G. Aloe saponaria** (5)
- **H. Phormium 'Bronze Baby'.** New Zealand flax (1)
- **I. Osteospermum fruticosum.** Trailing African daisy (6)
- **J. Oenothera speciosa (O. berlandieri).** Mexican evening primrose (8)
- **K. Teucrium chamaedrys 'Prostratum'.** Germander (8)
- **L. Zinnia grandiflora** (6)

TOP: *Cerastium tomentosum*
BOTTOM: *Limonium latifolium*

FRANKLY MODERN

An essentially straight entry path and angular planting beds reinforce the stripped-down, no-frills "modern" architecture of the 1950s. Yet the beds also relieve rigidity: because they impinge on either side of the walk, the journey to the front door describes a gentle curve.

Many of the plants are mounding or billowy, softening the straight lines of walk and bed edges—but the fortnight lily, New Zealand flax, and daylily offer spiky and fountain-like foliage clumps as well. Flowering starts in spring, with most perennials continuing through summer. Use this plan in full sun, in Zones 8, 9, 14–24.

PLANT LIST

A. Nandina domestica. Heavenly bamboo (1)

B. Rhaphiolepis (Raphiolepis) indica 'Indian Princess'.
India hawthorn (5+)

C. Berberis thunbergii 'Crimson Pygmy'.
Japanese barberry (2)

D. Phormium 'Apricot Queen'. New Zealand flax (1)

E. Dietes bicolor. Fortnight lily (1)

F. Hemerocallis 'Stella de Oro'. Daylily (2)

G. Salvia officinalis 'Berggarten'. Common sage (3)

H. Achillea millefolium, Galaxy strain. Common yarrow (4)

I. Limonium latifolium. Sea lavender (7)

J. Iberis sempervirens 'Snowflake'.
Evergreen candytuft (6)

K. Verbena tenuisecta 'Tapien Purple'. Moss verbena (8)

L. Teucrium chamaedrys 'Prostratum'. Germander (10)

M. Cerastium tomentosum. Snow-in-summer (6)

FRAMED BY IRREGULAR BEDS

Even if a perfectly straight entry walk is the best choice for your landscape, it doesn't have to look like a package ribbon tied across the yard. Here, curving beds hold relaxed plantings of shrubs and perennials, arranged in outward-sweeping drifts that de-emphasize the underlying severity. Leaf shapes vary, but all the plants are mounding, billowing, or spreading, offering a soft contrast to the straight walk. Warm flower colors play against cooler hues of white, silver, blue, and violet.

This plan is suited to Zones 3–6, 31, 32, 34, 35, 37, 39. To extend it to Zones 2, 40, and 41, replace A, B, C, and E in the list below with (respectively): beauty bush *(Kolkwitzia amabilis); Weigela florida* 'Variegata'; *Spiraea × bumalda* 'Goldmound'; and variegated purple moor grass *(Molinia caerulea* 'Variegata').

PLANT LIST

- **A. Buddleia davidii 'Black Knight'.** Butterfly bush (1)
- **B. Buddleia 'Lochinch'.** Butterfly bush (1)
- **C. Phlomis russeliana** (4+)
- **D. Miscanthus sinensis 'Purpurascens'.** Eulalia grass (1)
- **E. Pennisetum alopecuroides 'Hameln'.** Fountain grass (2)
- **F. Achillea 'Fireland'** (2)
- **G. Achillea filipendulina 'Coronation Gold.'** Fernleaf yarrow (4)
- **H. Achillea 'Moonshine'** (10)
- **I. Hemerocallis 'Happy Returns'** or other short yellow. Daylily (5)
- **J. Sedum 'Autumn Joy'** (Hylotelephium 'Autumn Joy') (9)
- **K. Salvia × superba 'May Night'** (11)
- **L. Chrysanthemum weyrichii 'White Bomb'** (Dendranthema weyrichii 'White Bomb') (10)
- **M. Artemisia stellerana 'Silver Brocade'.** Beach wormwood (17)

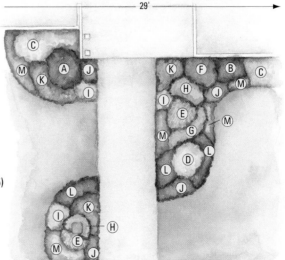

A FRONT YARD
"SECRET GARDEN"

Achillea, Galaxy strain

Why devote the front yard to grass or ground cover if you can instead enjoy an ever-changing tapestry of foliage and flowers? Especially if your lot is small, you can quite easily develop the plot bounded by sidewalk, driveway, and entry walk—a space usually given over to lawn and seldom walked upon.

In this design, a post-and-rail fence is a subtle foil for the plantings that flank and flow through it. Flower color starts in late winter with redbud and flowering quince, then continues with honeysuckle, daylily, and other plants until fall; foliage color adds interest for three or even all four seasons. All the plants thrive in Zones 4–9, 14–24.

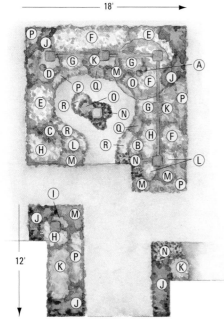

PLANT LIST

A. Cercis occidentalis.
Western redbud (1)

B. Calamagrostis × acutiflora 'Karl Foerster' ('Stricta').
Feather reed grass (1)

C. Chaenomeles 'Enchantress'.
Flowering quince (1)

D. Rhamnus alaternus 'Variegata'.
Italian buckthorn (1)

E. Teucrium fruticans.
Bush germander (5)

F. Abelia 'Edward Goucher'
(A. × grandiflora 'Edward Goucher') (5)

G. Lavandula angustifolia.
English lavender (3)

H. Achillea millefolium, Galaxy strain.
Common yarrow (10)

I. Lonicera × heckrottii.
Gold flame honeysuckle (1)

J. Mahonia aquifolium 'Compacta'.
Oregon grape (16)

K. Spiraea × bumalda 'Goldflame' (8)

L. Euphorbia characias wulfenii (3)

M. Salvia officinalis 'Berggarten'.
Common sage (8)

N. Verbena tenuisecta 'Tapien Purple'.
Moss verbena (12)

O. Hemerocallis, apricot pink cultivar.
Daylily (4)

P. Liriope spicata. Creeping lily turf (22)

Q. Sedum 'Autumn Joy'
(Hylotelephium 'Autumn Joy') (4)

R. Coreopsis verticillata 'Moonbeam'.
Threadleaf coreopsis (8)

NORTHWEST SECRET GARDEN

Aside from a few minor alterations in plant placement, our second "secret garden" is a replica of the design on the facing page. The most conspicuous difference is in the plants: this scheme is tailored for Pacific Northwest Zones 4–6, where coolness and moisture provide the ideal environment for a rich palette of choice plants.

Like the previous plan, this one offers a variety of foliage textures and colors for interest through all four seasons. Flower color, however, is concentrated more in the first half of the year. Lenten rose starts the floral procession in winter; the other flowering plants bloom throughout spring and into summer. An amelanchier in one corner gives small-tree height without density or gloom, and its leafless branches are attractive in winter.

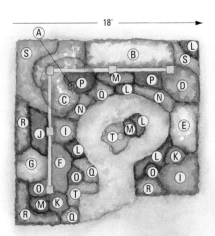

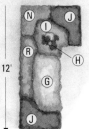

PLANT LIST

A. Amelanchier canadensis (1)

B. Rhododendron yakushimanum 'Ken Janeck' or 'Mist Maiden' (3)

C. Rhododendron (azalea) 'Gumpo' (3)

D. Paeonia suffruticosa. Tree peony (1)

E. Kalmia latifolia 'Elf'. Mountain laurel (2)

F. Spiraea × bumalda 'Goldflame' (2)

G. Pieris japonica 'Variegata'. Lily-of-the-valley shrub (3)

H. Clematis 'Hagley Hybrid' (1)

I. Geranium pratense. Meadow cranesbill (5)

J. Helleborus orientalis. Lenten rose (11)

K. Iris, Siberian, 'Flight of Butterflies' (2)

L. Iris, Pacific Coast native (16)

M. Hosta 'Krossa Regal' (6)

N. Hosta 'Gold Edger' (12)

O. Adenophora confusa. Lady bells (3)

P. Dicentra spectabilis. Common bleeding heart (2)

Q. Heuchera 'Pewter Veil' (4)

R. Alchemilla glaucescens (A. pubescens) (13)

S. Campanula portenschlagiana (C. muralis). Dalmatian bellflower (8)

T. Sagina subulata 'Aurea'. Scotch moss (twelve 3-inch squares, set 6 inches apart)

A FLOWERY WELCOME

Whether your front yard is spacious or small, you can dazzle your visitors and satisfy your gardening soul with plantings full of flowers.

If a driveway extends past the house to a garage farther back (as shown on this page), an entry walk can link drive and front door; the challenge here is to craft a planting striking enough to draw attention away from so much bare pavement. In the plan below—especially fine in Zones 3–6, 32–41—a gently winding path is flanked by irregular beds that give three-season color from flowers and foliage, including some fall leaf color.

If your front yard is shallow, planting it with lawn alone may make the space seem overexposed to the street. Add the illusion of depth by converting the entire yard to garden (as shown on the facing page), with converging paths from drive and sidewalk leading through a three-season flower fête. This scheme suits California Zones 8, 9, 14–24, where new homes are being built on ever smaller lots.

PLANT LIST

A. Acer palmatum 'Sango Kaku'.
Japanese maple (1)

B. Juniperus conferta.
Shore juniper (4+)

C. Berberis thunbergii 'Crimson Pygmy'.
Japanese barberry (6)

D. Clematis 'The President' (1)

E. Rosa 'White Dawn' (1)

F. Clethra alnifolia. Summersweet (1)

G. Viburnum opulus 'Compactum'.
European cranberry bush (2)

H. Spiraea × bumalda 'Goldflame' (2)

I. Chrysanthemum pacificum (Dendranthema pacificum). Gold and silver chrysanthemum (4)

J. Molinia caerulea 'Variegata'.
Variegated purple moor grass (2)

K. Achillea 'Fireland' (4)

L. Iris, Siberian, 'Fourfold White' (4)

M. Hemerocallis 'Happy Returns' or other short yellow. Daylily (9)

N. Rudbeckia fulgida sullivantii 'Goldsturm'.
Black-eyed Susan (3)

O. Salvia × superba 'May Night' (16)

P. Sedum 'Autumn Joy'
(Hylotelephium 'Autumn Joy') (7)

Q. Prunella grandiflora. Self-heal (28)

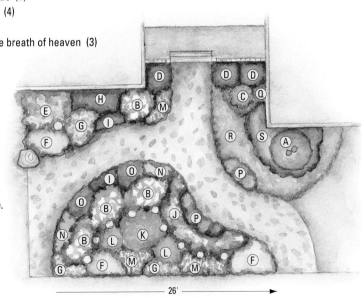

PLANT LIST

A. **Lagerstroemia 'Natchez' (multitrunked).** Crape myrtle (1)

B. **Rosa, such as 'First Light', 'Iceberg', 'Scentimental'** (4)

C. **Rosa 'The Fairy', as standard** (1)

D. **Coleonema album (Diosma alba, D. reevesii).** White breath of heaven (3)

E. **Escallonia × langleyensis 'Apple Blossom'** (1)

F. **Artemisia 'Powis Castle'** (6)

G. **Erigeron karvinskianus.**
Mexican daisy, Santa Barbara daisy (7)

H. **Penstemon × gloxinioides 'Firebird'.**
Border penstemon (4)

I. **Nepeta × faassenii.** Catmint (6)

J. **Erysimum 'Bowles Mauve'** (7)

K. **Achillea millefolium 'Appleblossom'.**
Common yarrow (3)

L. **Calamagrostis × acutiflora 'Karl Foerster' ('Stricta').**
Feather reed grass (2)

M. **Thymus praecox arcticus (T. serpyllum).**
Mother-of-thyme, creeping thyme (17)

N. **Stachys byzantina 'Silver Carpet'.** Lamb's ears (9)

O. **Geranium sanguineum.** Bloody cranesbill (3)

P. **Festuca ovina 'Glauca'.** Sheep fescue (21)

Q. **Liriope muscari 'Silvery Sunproof'.** Big blue lily turf (12)

R. **Potentilla neumanniana (P. tabernaemontanii, P. verna 'Nana').** Cinquefoil (40)

S. **Mahonia aquifolium 'Compacta'.** Oregon grape (12)

GRAND ENTRANCE

In bygone days, a curving drive was a standard feature of wealthy homes, typically sweeping under a porte-cochere where elegant carriages paused to discharge their occupants. Today, such drives usually lack the imposing overhead and are likely to serve only ordinary vehicles—and, perhaps, the occasional stretch limousine! Still, this design retains a bit of yesteryear's formality.

Color appears in all seasons, but aside from the striking display provided by azaleas and India hawthorn, the amount at any given moment is restrained. The sweet olive's blossoms, in fact, offer no particular show; instead, they proclaim their presence by their penetrating fragrance. All the plants are evergreen, appropriate for Western and Southeastern Zones 14–24, 28–31.

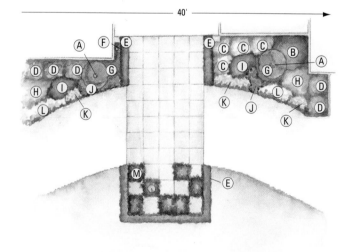

PLANT LIST

A. Osmanthus fragrans. Sweet olive (2)

B. Rhaphiolepis (Raphiolepis) indica 'Springtime'. India hawthorn (1)

C. Rhododendron (azalea) 'Gumpo' (4)

D. Rhododendron (azalea) 'Gumpo Pink' (5+)

E. Buxus microphylla koreana 'Tide Hill'. Korean boxwood (33)

F. Camellia sasanqua 'Mine-No-Yuki' ('White Doves') (1)

G. Liriope muscari 'Silvery Sunproof'. Big blue lily turf (18)

H. Nandina domestica 'Harbour Dwarf'. Heavenly bamboo (7)

I. Aspidistra elatior. Cast-iron plant (8)

J. Ajuga reptans. Carpet bugle (16)

K. Hemerocallis 'Stella de Oro'. Daylily (5)

L. Iberis sempervirens 'Snowflake'. Evergreen candytuft (11)

M. Ophiopogon japonicus. Mondo grass (24)

GRAND ENTRANCE, COUNTRY STYLE

In country-suburban properties, where land is more plentiful, the crescent drive offers an efficient entry for both cars and people. By running it through a garden, you make it interesting as well as practical. In this plan, the front yard could be shallow—with the fence set back several feet from a sidewalk—or quite deep, with the planted area located in a large expanse of lawn or ground cover. In either case, the low, open fence defines the planting while still letting parts of it flow through to the "outside."

Gardeners in chilly Zones 2–6, 32–41 will appreciate the hardiness of these plants: in fact, you may occasionally need to curb the spread of the yellowroot, loosestrife, and sweet woodruff. Flowers come and go during spring and summer; woody plants give good fall leaf color and some showy fruits.

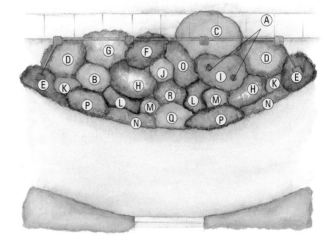

PLANT LIST

A. **Crataegus phaenopyrum.** Washington thorn (2)

B. **Cornus alba 'Elegantissima'.** Tatarian dogwood (1)

C. **Xanthorhiza simplicissima.** Yellowroot (3)

D. **Rosa 'Frau Dagmar Hartopp' ('Fru Dagmar Hastrup')** (3)

E. **Cotoneaster adpressus.** Creeping cotoneaster (7)

F. **Berberis thunbergii 'Atropurpurea'.** Red-leaf Japanese barberry (2)

G. **Lysimachia clethroides.** Gooseneck loosestrife (3)

H. **Astilbe × arendsii 'Bridal Veil'** (8)

I. **Athyrium filix-femina.** Lady fern (7)

J. **Iris, Siberian, light blue cultivar** (2)

K. **Hemerocallis, cream to light yellow cultivar.** Daylily (4)

L. **Epimedium × versicolor 'Sulphureum'.** Bishop's hat (9)

M. **Bergenia 'Abendglut' ('Evening Glow')** or **'Bressingham Ruby'** (3)

N. **Hosta 'Gold Edger'** (9)

O. **Galium odoratum.** Sweet woodruff (7)

P. **Thymus praecox arcticus 'Coccineus' (T. serpyllum 'Coccineus').** Mother-of-thyme, creeping thyme (20)

Q. **Sagina subulata 'Aurea'.** Scotch moss (fifteen 3-inch squares, set 6 inches apart)

R. **Chamaemelum nobile.** Chamomile (9)

Planting area: 40' x 12'

Weigela florida 'Variegata'

CONTEMPORARY GATED ENTRANCE

Where privacy or noise abatement is a priority, a substantial wall with an entry gate will give the desired result. With the wall set back from the street, the challenge is to come up with an attractive streetside planting that is uncluttered and easy to maintain. The focus is on the wall's public face. The overall design is formal—but the plants are largely informal, tied together by a tightly trimmed boxwood hedge. Foliage variegation and seasonal flowers on hydrangea and weigela, as well as blossoms on the magnolias, keep the planting looking interesting. This plan suits Zones 3–9, 14–17, 32–34, 39. To use it in Zones 2, 35–38, and 41, substitute Korean boxwood *(Buxus microphylla koreana)* and *Hydrangea arborescens* 'Annabelle' for the boxwood and hydrangea selections noted under A and B in the list below.

PLANT LIST

A. **Buxus microphylla japonica 'Green Beauty'.** Japanese boxwood (46+)

B. **Hydrangea macrophylla 'Tricolor'.** Bigleaf hydrangea (2)

C. **Magnolia kobus 'Wada's Memory'.** Kobus magnolia (2)

D. **Weigela florida 'Variegata'** (4+)

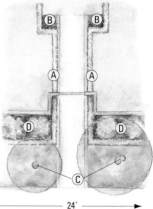

24'

A ROMANTIC PORTAL

What could be more romantic than a picket-fenced garden with an entry arbor bedecked in a tangle of roses and clematis? From a distance, its colorful extravagance proclaims "Welcome!" (if not also "Surrender!")—and once through the arbor, you're greeted by a cottage-garden array of flowering perennials.

Blossoms beguile you from spring through summer (and on into fall, in warmer zones). The color scheme is pastel—white,

pink, yellow—with the purple of the clematis and salvia for accent. Except for the lavandin, these plants will grow in Zones 2–9, 14–21, 32–41; the roses need winter protection in Zones 2, 3, 33–41. The lavandin (K in the list below) grows in Zones 4–24, 30–34, 39. In its place, use blue mist (*Caryopteris* × *clandonensis*) in Zones 3, 40, 41; use common wormwood (*Artemisia absinthium*) in Zones 2, 35–38.

PLANT LIST

A. **Rosa 'Climbing Iceberg'** (1)

B. **Clematis 'Etoile Violette'** (1)

C. **Rosa 'Awakening'** (2)

D. **Gypsophila paniculata 'Bristol Fairy'.** Baby's breath (3)

E. **Chrysanthemum × superbum 'Becky' (Leucanthemum maximum 'Becky').** Shasta daisy (7)

F. **Nepeta × faassenii 'Six Hills Giant'.** Catmint (5)

G. **Digitalis × mertonensis.** Foxglove (7)

H. **Salvia × superba 'May Night'** (7)

I. **Potentilla nepalensis 'Miss Willmott' ('Willmottiae').** Cinquefoil (11)

J. **Hemerocallis 'Stella de Oro'.** Daylily (7)

K. **Lavandula × intermedia 'Provence'.** Lavandin (16+)

Planting area: 34' x 9'

SURROUND THE WALL WITH GARDEN

Concrete paving and a stucco wall clearly mark this as a contemporary design, yet its roots are in Mediterranean antiquity, where concrete and plaster originated. These are hard, bright surfaces that look stark without the softening influence of plants—and the assortment shown here rises beautifully to the task. Mounded, irregular, loose, grassy, or frothy, they smooth sharp corners and gently blur straight edges.

Summer is the prime flowering season. The prevailing colors are blue, violet, yellow, and orange, with highlights of white and red. All the plants will succeed in Zones 3–7, 14–17, 32–34, 39. In Zones 35–38, 40, 41, you can substitute *Spiraea × bumalda* 'Goldmound' for phlomis (C in the list below), *Verbena canadensis* 'Homestead Purple' for moss verbena (G), and catmint (*Nepeta × faassenii*) for germander (I).

PLANT LIST

A. **Lonicera sempervirens.** Trumpet honeysuckle (2)

B. **Caryopteris × clandonensis.** Blue mist (2)

C. **Phlomis russeliana** (4+)

D. **Panicum virgatum 'Heavy Metal'.** Switch grass (3)

E. **Rudbeckia fulgida sullivantii 'Goldsturm'.** Black-eyed Susan (8)

F. **Limonium latifolium.** Sea lavender (12+)

G. **Verbena tenuisecta 'Tapien Purple'.** Moss verbena (18)

H. **Cerastium tomentosum.** Snow-in-summer (16+)

I. **Teucrium chamaedrys 'Prostratum'.** Germander (4)

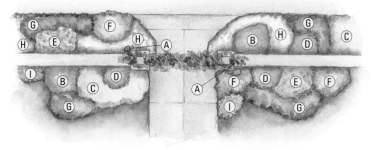

Planting area: 40' x 11'

UNDERSTATED ELEGANCE

A brick wall is the image of formality and restraint: when it separates public sidewalk from private yard, it clearly states "no trespassing." Nonetheless, its looks are often warm, not concrete-cold, conveying a welcome to those who are expected.

In keeping with this reserved yet friendly mood, the plants in the scheme shown here are elegant without being formally stiff. Contrasts in foliage texture make a three-season statement; flower color is at its peak in late spring, with the hydrangea carrying on into summer. The lightest afternoon shade suits all these plants, which perform best in Zones 3–9, 14–17, 32–34, 37–39. To suit the plan to Zones 40 and 41, substitute *Hydrangea arborescens* 'Annabelle' and *Rhododendron* (azalea) 'Orchid Lights' for the hydrangea and rhododendron suggested at right under C and D.

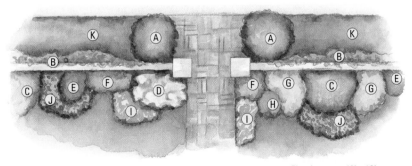

Planting area: 40' x 13'

PLANT LIST

A. **Berberis thunbergii 'Cherry Bomb'.** Japanese barberry (2)

B. **Parthenocissus quinquefolia.** Virginia creeper (2)

C. **Hydrangea serrata 'Preziosa'** (2)

D. **Rhododendron yakushimanum** (2)

E. **Iris, Siberian, 'Caesar's Brother'** (4)

F. **Astrantia major.** Masterwort (6)

G. **Alchemilla mollis.** Lady's-mantle (6)

H. **Bergenia 'Bressingham Ruby'** (1)

I. **Hosta 'Gold Edger'** (9)

J. **Epimedium alpinum.** Bishop's hat (7)

K. **Pachysandra terminalis.** Japanese spurge (20+)

FILLING IN THE BLANKS

In every suburban and rural home, gardeners face the same planting challenges: how to dress up a bare fence, a stark house wall, the empty ground beneath a tree, or a blank expanse of lawn or earth. The following 16 plans present a variety of schemes to address these often-difficult situations, with attention to the ever-present variables of sun, shade, rainfall patterns, and overall climate, be it mild or harsh.

FLORIFEROUS FENCEROW

Boundary fences are a fact of suburban life—but to the gardener's eye, even the most attractive fence can look a bit stark without some sort of horticultural costuming. In the plan shown below, a weathered wooden fence is a backdrop for a lush-looking planting that needs only moderate water, yet provides good color from spring into fall. This scheme is intended for a sunny location in California's Zones 14–24, where winters are mild, summers are warm to hot, and water is at a premium. It's a relatively low-maintenance planting: one round of cleanup and discretionary pruning in winter will prepare it for a return engagement the next year.

PLANT LIST

A. Anisodontea capensis. Cape mallow (1)
B. Erysimum 'Bowles Mauve' (1)
C. Verbena bonariensis (1)
D. Penstemon × gloxinioides 'Sour Grapes'. Border penstemon (3)
E. Agapanthus orientalis 'Albus'. Lily-of-the-Nile (1)
F. Erigeron karvinskianus. Mexican daisy, Santa Barbara daisy (4+)

G. Helichrysum italicum (H. angustifolium). Curry plant (2)
H. Aloe saponaria (2)
I. Osteospermum fruticosum. Trailing African daisy (4+)
J. Scaevola 'Mauve Clusters' (2)
K. Convolvulus mauritanicus. Ground morning glory (2)
L. Stachys byzantina 'Silver Carpet'. Lamb's ears (5+)

Planting area: 22' x 6'

BEAUTIFUL BOUNDARY

Some fences are quite open in structure, marking boundaries without creating visual barriers—as here, where a post-and-rail fence defines the edge of a cultivated garden while allowing a clear view into the wild meadow beyond. Given regular moisture and a full-sun location, this varied floral assortment delivers a summer's worth of color. The plants are all herbaceous perennials, dying back to the ground or to low tufts of foliage when the growing season ends. A quick cleanup in late winter readies the planting for spring growth. This plan is especially well suited to Zones 32–41 but will also succeed in Zones 2–9, 14–21.

PLANT LIST

A. Hibiscus moscheutos 'Blue River'. Perennial hibiscus (1)

B. Echinacea purpurea 'Magnus'. Purple coneflower (4+)

C. Liatris spicata 'Kobold'. Gayfeather (2)

D. Geranium psilostemon (2+)

E. Hemerocallis 'Black-eyed Stella'. Daylily (2)

F. Coreopsis grandiflora 'Early Sunrise' (4+)

G. Salvia × superba 'May Night' (7+)

H. Chrysanthemum × superbum 'Snow Lady' (Leucanthemum maximum 'Snow Lady'). Shasta daisy (3)

I. Nepeta × faassenii. Catmint (6+)

J. Iberis sempervirens. Evergreen candytuft (5)

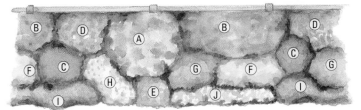

Planting area: 22' x 6'

TOP: *Nepeta × faassenii*
BOTTOM: *Liatris spicata* 'Kobold'

Campanula poscharskyana

SHADED FENCE FOR THE SUNBELT

Over much of California's Zones 14–24 and throughout the Southeast's Zones 31 and 32, summers are warm to hot. In these areas, summer shade is a welcome relief for people, but it may not always suit plants. The assortment suggested here, though, is perfectly at home in very light shade all day, or with a little morning sun followed by light shade in the afternoon. There's no peak season for flower color, but you do enjoy it in all seasons, from winter's camellia through fall's Japanese anemone and the last of the impatiens. Heuchera, lily turf, and Japanese forest grass provide subtle but steady foliage color throughout the growing season.

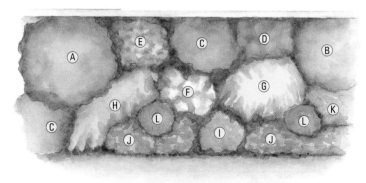

Planting area: 20' x 8'

PLANT LIST

A. **Camellia japonica 'Nuccio's Pearl'** (1)

B. **Rhododendron (azalea) 'George Lindley Taber'** (1)

C. **Rhododendron (azalea) 'Hinodegiri'** (2)

D. **Anemone × hybrida.** Japanese anemone (3)

E. **Digitalis × mertonensis.** Foxglove (4)

F. **Helleborus argutifolius (H. lividus corsicus).** Corsican hellebore (2)

G. **Hakonechloa macra 'Aureola'.** Japanese forest grass (3)

H. **Liriope muscari 'Variegata'.** Big blue lily turf (5)

I. **Heuchera 'Palace Purple'** (2)

J. **Ajuga reptans.** Carpet bugle (14+)

K. **Campanula poscharskyana.** Serbian bellflower (3+)

L. **Impatiens wallerana** (annuals, in pots)

SHADED FENCE FOR COLDER REGIONS

Where houses are fairly close together, shade is sure to affect plantings along a fence or wall—and those areas will be even dimmer and cooler (and for more hours of the day) if the houses are tall and mature trees grow nearby. Nonetheless, you can still enjoy a visually interesting planting punctuated by floral color. The scheme shown here works well in Zones 3–6, 32–41, where the plants will thrive in light to moderate shade all day if given regular watering. Summer is the most colorful season: the foliage of bergenia and hosta is at its most striking, and the meadow rue, masterwort, astilbe, and summersweet are all in bloom.

Convallaria majalis

PLANT LIST

A. **Clethra alnifolia.** Summersweet (1)

B. **Rhododendron 'PJM'** (2)

C. **Thalictrum rochebrunianum.** Meadow rue (6)

D. **Astrantia major.** Masterwort (5+)

E. **Polystichum acrostichoides.** Christmas fern (4)

F. **Hosta sieboldiana 'Elegans'** (2)

G. **Astilbe simplicifolia 'Sprite'** (5)

H. **Bergenia 'Bressingham Ruby'** (2)

I. **× Heucherella tiarelloides 'Pink Frost'** (4)

J. **Convallaria majalis.** Lily-of-the-valley (8+)

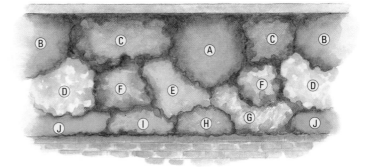

Planting area: 20' x 8'

Sedum 'Autumn Joy'

PICTURE PERFECT

Plantings along a house have a softening effect on the landscape, creating a transition from manmade structure to natural environment. Where these foundation plantings are easily seen from a window, you'll want to create an especially eye-pleasing scheme. One such "picture window" design is shown here, offering colorful flowers and foliage from earliest spring into autumn. This assortment prefers regular moisture but will forgive occasional lapses. It may be satisfied by natural rainfall in Zones 32–39, but you'll surely need to provide some water in Zones 3–9, 14–16, 18–21. Substitute *Geranium* 'Ann Folkard' for *G.* × *magnificum* (E in the list below) and the plan can also be enjoyed in Zones 2, 40, and 41.

PLANT LIST

A. **Prunus** × **cistena.**
   Purple-leaf sand cherry (1)

B. **Paeonia suffruticosa.** Tree peony (3)

C. **Gypsophila paniculata.** Baby's breath (2)

D. **Hemerocallis, yellow cultivar.** Daylily (8)

E. **Geranium** × **magnificum** (4)

F. **Geranium himalayense (G. grandiflorum)**
   'Birch Double' ('Plenum') (3)

G. **Heuchera 'Palace Purple'** (3)

H. **Sedum 'Autumn Joy'**
   (Hylotelephium 'Autumn Joy') (2)

I. **Salvia** × **superba 'May Night'** (10+)

J. **Dianthus** × **allwoodii 'Aqua'.** Pink (8)

K. **Potentilla nepalensis 'Miss Willmott'**
   ('Willmottiae'). Cinquefoil (8)

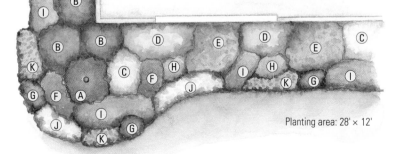

Planting area: 28' × 12'

VIEW FROM A WINDOW

In regions where water is scant or expensive, the gardener's challenge is to create plantings with limited thirst. In California's Zones 8, 9, 14–24, rainfall may take care of winter water needs, but the warm months are typically too dry to support a varied garden without some assistance from the hose. The scheme shown here follows the same plot plan as "Picture Perfect" (facing page), but it uses plants that will prosper with less than regular watering. Consistent color comes from a variety of plants with gray, yellow, and purplish foliage. Flower color is present from spring into fall, but it crests in the summer display depicted above.

Gazania 'Burgundy'

PLANT LIST

A. **Buddleia davidii 'Dark Knight'.** Butterfly bush (1)

B. **Phlomis fruticosa.** Jerusalem sage (3)

C. **Lavandula × intermedia 'Provence'.** Lavandin (2)

D. **Pennisetum setaceum 'Rubrum'.** Fountain grass (5)

E. **Coleonema pulchrum 'Sunset Gold' (Diosma pulchra 'Sunset Gold').** Pink breath of heaven (2)

F. **Achillea taygetea** (5)

G. **Convolvulus cneorum.** Bush morning glory (3)

H. **Kniphofia uvaria 'Little Maid'.** Red-hot poker (2)

I. **Erigeron karvinskianus.** Mexican daisy, Santa Barbara daisy (6+)

J. **Verbena tenuisecta 'Tapien Purple'.** Moss verbena (7)

K. **Gazania 'Burgundy'** (10)

Brunnera macrophylla

SHADEMASTERS

One or more sides of your house are bound to be shady. The eastern and western faces may have half-day shade, but the northern exposures (as well as any walls shaded by trees or buildings) will be at least partly in shadow all day long. And if a shaded wall jags in and out rather than proceeding in an unbroken line, the shadows will be especially deep and cool in the nooks thus created. Fortunately, you needn't consign these darker regions to ivy and moss. The grouping illustrated below offers both subtle foliage color and periodic floral color. The birdbath rises from a "pool" of blue scaevola blossoms, but you can certainly construct a real pond if you prefer. With regular watering, this planting will thrive in all-day light shade in Zones 8, 9, 14–24; by substituting bishop's hat (*Epimedium × rubrum* 'Snow Queen') for vancouveria (J in the list below) and carpet bugle *(Ajuga reptans)* for scaevola (K), you can achieve virtually the same effect in Zones 4–7, 32, and 33.

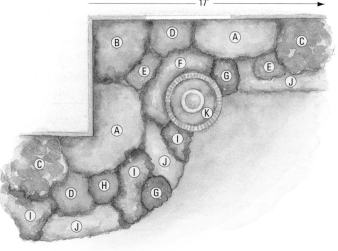

PLANT LIST

A. Rhododendron (azalea) 'Gumpo' (4)

B. Aucuba japonica. Japanese aucuba (1)

C. Hydrangea macrophylla 'Tricolor'. Bigleaf hydrangea (2)

D. Brunnera macrophylla (2)

E. Adenophora confusa. Lady bells (4)

F. Liriope muscari 'Variegata'. Big blue lily turf (6)

G. Bergenia 'Bressingham Ruby' (2)

H. Iris foetidissima. Gladwin iris (1)

I. × Heucherella tiarelloides 'Pink Frost' (7+)

J. Vancouveria hexandra (7+)

K. Scaevola 'Mauve Clusters' (3)

HOT SPOTS

Spend a bit of time in the sun near a south-facing house wall, and soon you're gasping for breath. But while the environment may be too hot for most people to handle comfortably, a variety of good-looking plants thrive in just these spots. This gathering features natives of regions where blistering summers are the norm; given the same conditions in your garden, they'll feel right at home. (Flowering is at its peak in summer, too.) Try this plan in desert Zones 12 and 13, as well as in Zones 14, 18–21.

PLANT LIST

A. **Lagerstroemia 'Zuni'.** Crape myrtle (1)

B. **Teucrium fruticans.** Bush germander (3)

C. **Nerium oleander 'Petite Salmon'.** Oleander (3)

D. **Punica granatum 'Nana'.** Dwarf pomegranate (3)

E. **Tecomaria capensis 'Aurea' (Tecoma capensis 'Aurea').** Cape honeysuckle (1)

F. **Pittosporum tobira 'Wheeler's Dwarf'.** Tobira (3+)

G. **Dietes vegeta.** Fortnight lily (2)

H. **Erigeron karvinskianus.** Mexican daisy, Santa Barbara daisy (5)

I. **Santolina chamaecyparissus.** Lavender cotton (2)

J. **Achillea taygetea** (3)

K. **Teucrium chamaedrys 'Prostratum'.** Germander (8)

L. **Oenothera speciosa (O. berlandieri).** Mexican evening primrose (3)

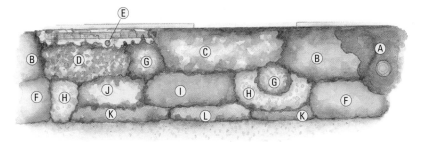

Planting area: 37' x 8'

Helleborus orientalis

VENERABLE SHELTER

Though a mature deciduous tree is a treasure to be cherished, it often sits squarely in a spot where you'd also like to establish an ornamental planting. Some trees (such as sweet gum, *Liquidambar*) have aggressive surface root systems that will ultimately defeat your efforts. But given a reasonably deep-rooted tree like the scarlet oak *(Quercus coccinea)* shown here, you can literally have it all. The limbs extend to shelter a potpourri of shade-tolerant plants that reach a crescendo of color in summer, brightening the garden with both flowers and non-green foliage. These plants will succeed in Zones 3–6, 32–41.

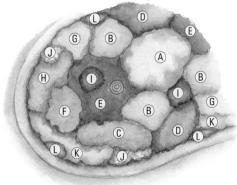

Planting area: 20' x 16'

PLANT LIST

A. Aruncus dioicus (A. sylvester).
Goat's beard (2)

B. Alchemilla mollis.
Lady's-mantle (8+)

C. Hakonechloa macra 'Aureola'.
Japanese forest grass (4)

D. Helleborus orientalis.
Lenten rose (6+)

E. Brunnera macrophylla (8+)

F. Thalictrum aquilegifolium.
Meadow rue (3)

G. Corydalis lutea (6+)

H. Astilbe simplicifolia 'Sprite' (5)

I. Athyrium filix-femina.
Lady fern (2)

J. Galax urceolata (4)

K. Hosta 'Gold Edger' (10+)

**L. Endymion non-scriptus
(Scilla non-scripta).**
English bluebell (16)

DRY-SHADE DENIZENS

Shade and dryness characterize the conditions of many a forest floor, where the typical flora features plenty of greenery and few or no blossoms. The same basic scheme holds true in dry, low-light garden spots: you can choose a variety of green shades and variegations to create a subtle tapestry, but any color will serve as an exclamation point. The planting shown above adorns the ground beneath a Japanese scholar tree *(Sophora japonica).*

The variegated leaves of Japanese aucuba, osmanthus, and lily turf add light to the composition; red tints in the foliage of heavenly bamboo and bishop's hat contribute a touch of color. Notable flower color comes just from lily turf, bishop's hat, and cinquefoil. Use this grouping in Zones 4–9, 14–17, 32, and 33. Gardeners in Zones 10, 18–21 can substitute dwarf periwinkle *(Vinca minor)* for bishop's hat (G in the list below).

PLANT LIST

A. **Aucuba japonica 'Picturata'**
('Aureo-maculata'). Japanese aucuba (2)

B. **Osmanthus heterophyllus 'Variegatus'.**
Holly-leaf osmanthus (3)

C. **Mahonia aquifolium 'Compacta'.**
Oregon grape (12)

D. **Nandina domestica 'Harbour Dwarf'.**
Heavenly bamboo (9+)

E. **Iris foetidissima.** Gladwin iris (5)

F. **Liriope muscari 'Silvery Sunproof'.**
Big blue lily turf (7)

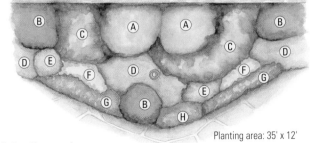

Planting area: 35' x 12'

G. **Epimedium × rubrum.**
Bishop's hat (10)

H. **Potentilla recta 'Macrantha' (P. recta 'Warrenii', P. warrenii).** Cinquefoil (4)

BENEATH A COAST LIVE OAK

California gardeners in Zones 7–9, 14–24 treasure mature specimens of the coast live oak *(Quercus agrifolia)*, the signature tree of the state's oak-dotted hillsides. With the spread of housing into their native territory, many of these trees now find themselves in gardens, where they often receive watering during their accustomed summer-dry period—a situation that ultimately proves fatal for them. To garden successfully with a mature (and formerly wild) coast live oak, you must keep off-season water away from its roots as much as possible. The plan shown here maintains a 10-foot buffer zone of gravel between tree trunk and planting, and it concentrates on unthirsty plants that can be given the occasional summer drink via a drip-irrigation system that largely bypasses the oak. There's no mass color display, but flowers dot the planting in winter and spring.

Planting area: 37' x 22'

PLANT LIST

A. **Garrya elliptica 'James Roof'.** Coast silktassel (3)

B. **Ribes sanguineum.** Pink winter currant (3)

C. **Rhamnus californica 'Seaview'.** Coffeeberry (4)

D. **Cotoneaster dammeri 'Lowfast'.** Bearberry cotoneaster (10)

E. **Mahonia aquifolium 'Compacta'.** Oregon grape (16)

F. **Polystichum munitum.** Sword fern (2)

G. **Bergenia crassifolia.** Winter-blooming bergenia (4)

H. **Iris, Pacific Coast native** (9)

I. **Heuchera 'Santa Ana Cardinal'.** Coral bells (4)

J. **Duchesnea indica.** Indian mock strawberry (10)

A CANOPY BED

Where two or more trees join forces to shelter an area, you can craft a fairly ambitious garden of shade-loving plants. Here, two garden-compatible trees—a locust and a dogwood—spread their limbs above a good-sized plot, casting mottled shadows over a diverse planting that sports variegated or colored foliage throughout the growing season and provides bursts of flower color from spring through fall. Both the plants and the two trees perform best with regular water, in Zones 4–9, 14, 15, 32.

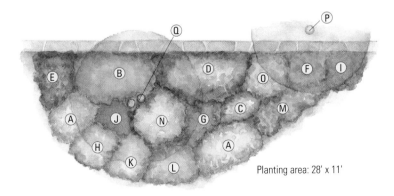

Planting area: 28' x 11'

PLANT LIST

A. Alchemilla mollis. Lady's-mantle (3)

B. Anemone × hybrida 'Honorine Jobert'. Japanese anemone (5)

C. Molinia caerulea 'Variegata'. Variegated purple moor grass (1)

D. Berberis thunbergii 'Atropurpurea'. Red-leaf Japanese barberry (2)

E. Bergenia crassifolia. Winter-blooming bergenia (3)

F. Digitalis purpurea. Common foxglove (4)

G. Helleborus argutifolius (H. lividus corsicus). Corsican hellebore (3)

H. Hosta 'Chinese Sunrise' (3)

I. Hosta sieboldiana 'Elegans' (1)

J. Iris foetidissima. Gladwin iris (2)

K. Lamium maculatum 'White Nancy'. Dead nettle (3)

L. Liriope muscari. Big blue lily turf (3)

M. Liriope muscari 'Variegata'. Big blue lily turf (4)

N. Thalictrum aquilegifolium. Meadow rue (3)

O. Thalictrum rochebrunianum 'Lavender Mist'. Meadow rue (3)

P. Cornus × rutgersensis 'Aurora'. Stellar dogwood (1)

Q. Robinia pseudoacacia 'Frisia'. Black locust (1)

Santolina chamaecyparissus

DESERT ISLAND

As originally conceived, the "island bed" was a sizable plant grouping afloat in a sea of turf. But in semiarid regions (where seas of turf are a troublesome extravagance), there's no reason an island can't be an oasis of flowers and foliage in an otherwise dry expanse. This grouping gets its vivid color from both blossoms and an abundance of non-green foliage; the display is at its showiest from midspring to midsummer. The plants coexist swimmingly in California's dry-summer Zones 14–24. In the coastal zones, they may sail through the growing season with no supplemental water; in hotter inland zones, they'll probably need an occasional summer drink from the hose.

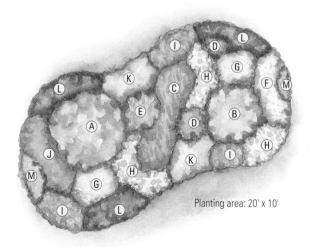

Planting area: 20' x 10'

PLANT LIST

A. Cistus ladanifer. Crimson-spot rockrose (1)

B. Phlomis fruticosa. Jerusalem sage (1)

C. Lavandula × intermedia 'Provence'. Lavandin (2)

D. Euphorbia characias wulfenii (2)

E. Phormium 'Yellow Wave'. New Zealand flax (1)

F. Convolvulus cneorum. Bush morning glory (3)

G. Centranthus ruber 'Albus'. Jupiter's beard (4)

H. Erigeron karvinskianus. Mexican daisy, Santa Barbara daisy (8)

I. Oenothera speciosa (O. berlandieri). Mexican evening primrose (8)

J. Penstemon 'Garnet' (4)

K. Santolina chamaecyparissus. Lavender cotton (4)

L. Verbena tenuisecta 'Tapien Purple'. Moss verbena (11)

M. Aloe saponaria (3)

WATER-THRIFTY ISLAND

Though it follows the same plan as our "Desert Island" (facing page), this water-thrifty grouping is intended especially for Zones 32–41, where gardens receive some summer rainfall but not always enough to sustain plants needing regular moisture. Flower color begins in late spring with the false indigo, then continues on into summer (peaking in July and August) and maintains a good display well into the autumn, weather permitting.

Given periodic watering during summer, this planting will also succeed in Zones 3–7, 14–17.

Asclepias tuberosa

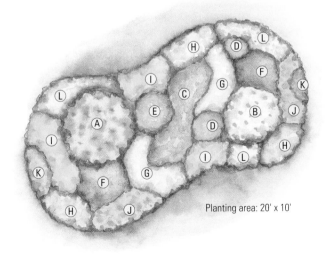

Planting area: 20' x 10'

PLANT LIST

A. **Echinacea purpurea 'Magnus'.** Purple coneflower (7)
B. **Echinacea purpurea 'White Swan'** (5)
C. **Baptisia australis.** Blue false indigo (2)
D. **Asclepias tuberosa.** Butterfly weed (2)
E. **Panicum virgatum 'Heavy Metal'.** Switch grass (1)
F. **Caryopteris × clandonensis.** Blue mist (2)
G. **Achillea ptarmica 'The Pearl'** (7)
H. **Achillea tomentosa 'King George'.** Woolly yarrow (9)
I. **Coreopsis grandiflora 'Early Sunrise'** (9)
J. **Gaillardia × grandiflora 'Goblin'.** Blanket flower (7)
K. **Sedum 'Autumn Joy' (Hylotelephium 'Autumn Joy')** (5)
L. **Cerastium tomentosum.** Snow-in-summer (9)

COOL ISLAND

From spring through summer, this soothing oasis presents an ever-changing array of flowers in tones of blue, purple, white, and pink—the perfect cooling antidote for the midsummer blahs. When flowering wanes, colored and variegated foliage keeps the planting interesting. All the plants will succeed with regular (but not lavish) watering in Zones 3–9, 32, and 33. Gardeners in Zones 14–21 can enjoy the plan as well if *Dictamnus albus* 'Albiflorus' and *D. a.* 'Purpureus' are replaced with *Liatris spicata* 'Alba' and *L. s.* 'Kobold'.

Aster × *frikartii* 'Mönch'

PLANT LIST

A. **Achillea millefolium 'White Beauty'.** Yarrow (4)

B. **Ajuga reptans 'Purpurea'.** Carpet bugle (8)

C. **Aster** × **frikartii 'Mönch'** (4)

D. **Cerastium tomentosum.** Snow-in-summer (3)

E. **Dictamnus albus 'Albiflorus'.** Gas plant (1)

F. **Dictamnus albus 'Purpureus'.** Gas plant (1)

G. **Gaura lindheimeri** (2)

H. **Hemerocallis 'Little Grapette'.** Daylily (5)

I. **Heuchera 'Palace Purple'** (4)

J. **Hibiscus syriacus 'Diana'.** Rose of Sharon (1)

K. **Iberis sempervirens 'Snowflake'.** Evergreen candytuft (8)

L. **Iris, tall bearded, 'Pallida Variegata' ('Zebra')** (4)

M. **Iris, tall bearded, 'Titan's Glory'** (4)

N. **Iris, tall bearded, 'Stepping Out'** (3)

O. **Limonium latifolium.** Sea lavender (6)

P. **Liriope muscari 'Silvery Sunproof'.** Big blue lily turf (8)

Q. **Nepeta** × **faassenii.** Catmint (3)

R. **Salvia** × **superba 'East Friesland'** (13)

S. **Scabiosa caucasica.** Pincushion flower (4)

T. **Stachys byzantina 'Silver Carpet'.** Lamb's ears (11)

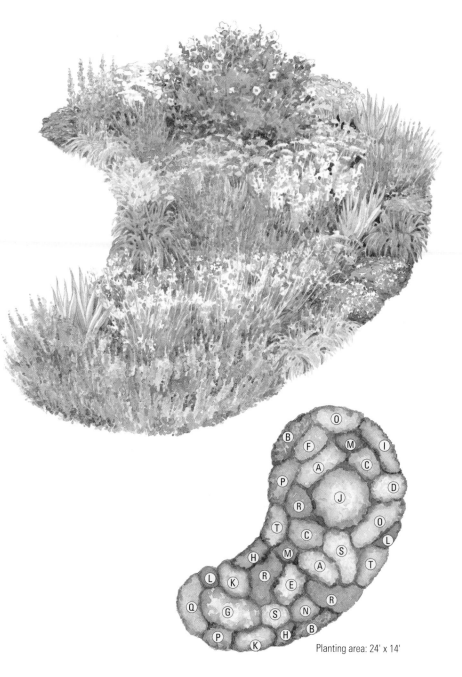

Planting area: 24' x 14'

Echinacea purpurea

GRAND ISLAND

Where space is not an issue, set this island into your lawn for a Really Big Show. It's centered with a sinuous "spine" of shrubs in varying sizes; plantings on either side of this backbone flow outward to the perimeter. The effect is grand indeed, with flowers and foliage offering interest from early spring clear into fall. Due to its width, the island is a bit awkward to maintain—you have no choice but to wade into it to reach the interior plants. When you see it in its glory, though, you'll know the extra work is worth the effort! All the plants need routine summer moisture and are well suited to summer-rainfall Zones 32–35, 37, and 39; they'll also thrive (with watering from you) in Zones 3–9, 14–17. To extend the planting into Zones 2, 36, 38, 40, and 41, replace the butterfly bush (C in the list at right) with blue false indigo (*Baptisia australis*) or lead plant (*Amorpha canescens*).

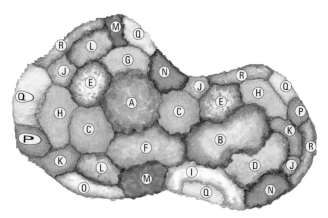

Planting area: 35' x 22'

PLANT LIST

A. Hibiscus syriacus 'Aphrodite'. Rose of Sharon (1)

B. Weigela florida 'Variegata' (2)

C. Buddleia davidii 'Nanho Purple'. Butterfly bush (2)

D. Spiraea × bumalda 'Goldflame' (2)

E. Malva moschata 'Alba'. Musk mallow (2)

F. Helictotrichon sempervirens (Avena sempervirens). Blue oat grass (5)

G. Liatris scariosa 'White Spire'. Gayfeather (3)

H. Achillea millefolium, pink cultivar (e.g. 'Appleblossom', 'Heidi'). Common yarrow (7)

I. Achillea ptarmica 'The Pearl' (6)

J. Hemerocallis 'Hyperion'. Daylily (6)

K. Liatris spicata 'Kobold'. Gayfeather (7)

L. Echinacea purpurea 'Magnus'. Purple coneflower (10)

M. Aster × frikartii 'Mönch' (6)

N. Salvia × superba 'May Night' (11)

O. Salvia × sylvestris 'Schneehügel' ('Snowhill') (6)

P. Sedum 'Autumn Joy' (Hylotelephium 'Autumn Joy') (5)

Q. Coreopsis auriculata 'Nana' (17)

R. Nepeta × faassenii. Catmint (13)

ALL THE GARDEN A PATIO

Acanthus mollis

If the thought of mowing even a small lawn is anathema to you, consider transforming your 30- by 40-foot yard into a patio garden. In this design, the entire space is visible from the house, drawing you outdoors to experience the plantings close up. The 5-foot-square pavers are arranged to form several intimate nooks, where benches or chaises longues invite you to linger and enjoy the blossoms of bougainvillea and bright perennials (color is at its height in early summer). Beneath the shade of a Brazilian butterfly tree, a tranquil pool offers a soothing note—and a home for gleaming koi, if you're so inclined. Use this planting scheme in Zones 12, 13, 15–17, 19, 22–28.

PLANT LIST

A. Bougainvillea 'California Gold' ('Sunset') (2)

B. Bougainvillea 'Tahitian Dawn' (2)

C. × Fatshedera lizei (1)

D. Bauhinia forficata (B. corniculata, B. candicans). Brazilian butterfly tree (1)

E. Yucca gloriosa. Spanish dagger (1)

F. Osmanthus fragrans. Sweet olive (3)

G. Feijoa sellowiana. Pineapple guava (3)

H. Pittosporum tobira 'Wheeler's Dwarf'. Tobira (11)

I. Punica granatum 'Nana'. Dwarf pomegranate (7)

J. Abelia 'Edward Goucher' (Abelia × grandiflora 'Edward Goucher') (3)

K. Rhaphiolepis (Raphiolepis) indica 'Clara'. India hawthorn (2)

L. Dietes bicolor. Fortnight lily (3)

M. Agapanthus orientalis. Lily-of-the-Nile (3)

N. Agapanthus 'Peter Pan'. Lily-of-the-Nile (10)

O. Hemerocallis, large yellow cultivar. Daylily (6)

P. Hemerocallis 'Black-eyed Stella'. Daylily (5)

Q. Liriope muscari 'Silvery Sunproof'. Big blue lily turf (9)

R. Ophiopogon japonicus. Mondo grass (24)

S. Acanthus mollis. Bear's breech (4)

T. Erigeron karvinskianus. Mexican daisy, Santa Barbara daisy (15)

U. Achillea tomentosa 'King George'. Woolly yarrow (14)

V. Verbena rigida 'Flame' (7)

W. Verbena tenuisecta 'Tapien Purple'. Moss verbena (20)

X. Ajuga reptans. Carpet bugle (24)

Y. Teucrium chamaedrys 'Prostratum'. Germander (22)

Z. Hedera helix 'Glacier'. English ivy (12 starts)

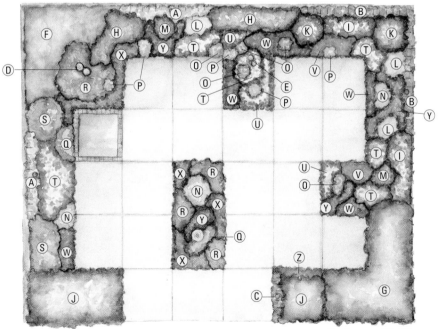

Planting area: 40' x 30'

KEEP IT SIMPLE

Though this design calls for nineteen different plants, it doesn't have a busy look: it gives the impression of unity and simplicity. Shrubs are its mainstay, and the mass planting of just a few sorts helps draw the garden together. Thanks to the profusion of rhododendrons and azaleas, the flower show is most striking in late spring, but bloom begins earlier on, with late winter's flowering quince and the redbud's flashy pink early-spring display. Even when flowers are not present, the garden has a subtle sparkle from colorful and variegated foliage on redbud, heather, iris, lily-of-the-valley shrub, and several other plants. Zones 4–6, 14–17 are best for this plan, but it will also succeed in Zones 34, 37, and 39 if you make a few changes: substitute locally successful rhododendrons and azaleas for those suggested under E through I in the list below, use carpet bugle *(Ajuga reptans)* in place of blue star creeper (R), and eliminate the gladwin iris (O).

PLANT LIST

A. **Acer palmatum 'Sango Kaku'.** Japanese maple (1)

B. **Cercis canadensis 'Forest Pansy'.** Eastern redbud (2)

C. **Chaenomeles 'Toyo Nishiki'.** Flowering quince (1)

D. **Clematis 'Henryi'** (2)

E. **Rhododendron 'Lem's Monarch'** ('Pink Walloper') (1)

F. **Rhododendron 'Unique'** (1)

G. **Rhododendron 'Moonstone'** (1)

H. **Rhododendron 'PJM'** (6)

I. **Rhododendron (azalea) 'Gumpo'** (4)

J. **Euonymus fortunei 'Emerald Gaiety'** (8)

K. **Pieris japonica 'Variegata'.** Lily-of-the-valley shrub (3)

L. **Calluna vulgaris 'Blazeaway'.** Heather (5)

M. **Hosta 'Frances Williams'** (3)

N. **Hosta 'Hadspen Blue'** (4)

O. **Iris foetidissima 'Variegata'.** Gladwin iris (2)

P. **Helleborus orientalis.** Lenten rose (5)

Q. **Sagina subulata 'Aurea'.** Scotch moss (3-inch squares, set 6 inches apart)

R. **Pratia pedunculata (Laurentia fluviatilis, Isotoma fluviatilis).** Blue star creeper (twelve 3-inch squares, set 6 inches apart)

S. **Equisetum hyemale.** Horsetail (1, in pot in pool)

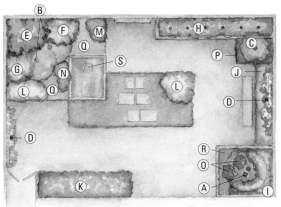

Planting area: 30' x 20'

SUMMER SHOWPIECE

Jam packed with color, this jewel-like planting is a mere 20 feet deep and 30 feet wide. Stroll along the path that leads throughout the garden, pausing to admire each plant; or, for prolonged contemplation, take advantage of a sheltered gazebo or *plein air* bench. The planting is designed for chilly-winter Zones 3–6, 32–41, where summer is the prime season for floral splendor and outdoor living. The flowering year, though, begins in spring, with the early show of serviceberry, wisteria, sand cherry, and lily-of-the-valley followed by the later spring blossoms of cranberry bush, mountain laurel, and Siberian iris.

PLANT LIST

A. **Amelanchier × grandiflora.** Apple serviceberry (1)

B. **Wisteria sinensis.** Chinese wisteria (1)

C. **Prunus × cistena.** Purple-leaf sand cherry (2)

D. **Viburnum opulus 'Compactum'.** European cranberry bush (2)

E. **Kalmia latifolia.** Mountain laurel (2)

F. **Kalmia latifolia 'Elf'.** Mountain laurel (2)

G. **Spiraea × bumalda 'Goldflame'** (4)

H. **Spiraea japonica 'Shirobana' ('Shibori')** (3)

I. **Berberis thunbergii.** Japanese barberry (4)

J. **Berberis thunbergii 'Crimson Pygmy'.** Japanese barberry (1)

K. **Potentilla fruticosa 'Abbotswood'.** Cinquefoil (3)

L. **Calamagrostis × acutiflora 'Karl Foerster' ('Stricta').** Feather reed grass (1)

M. **Gypsophila paniculata 'Bristol Fairy'.** Baby's breath (3)

N. **Geranium himalayense (G. grandiflorum) 'Birch Double' ('Plenum')** (8)

O. **Coreopsis verticillata 'Moonbeam'.** Threadleaf coreopsis (4)

P. **Penstemon digitalis 'Husker Red'** (4)

Q. **Iris, Siberian, blue cultivar (e.g. 'Orville Fay')** (4)

R. **Heuchera 'Palace Purple'** (7)

S. **Nepeta × faassenii.** Catmint (4)

T. **Prunella grandiflora.** Self-heal (16)

U. **Campanula portenschlagiana (C. muralis).** Dalmatian bellflower (5)

V. **Thymus praecox arcticus 'Coccineum' (T. serpyllum 'Coccineum').** Mother-of-thyme, creeping thyme (8)

W. **Convallaria majalis.** Lily-of-the-valley (12)

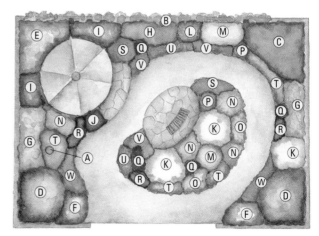

Planting area: 30' x 20'

Pacific Coast native iris

A SECRET-GARDEN PATIO

From inside the house, you see a bit of paving, a stunning actinidia vine on a trellis, and just a hint of something beyond. Venturing outside, you discover a leafy, secluded retreat screened from the house yet still linked to it by the flow of paving and plantings. The look is serene, not flashy: color comes and goes with the seasons, sparking the garden here and there. Varied foliage textures and colors sustain interest for most of the year. The plan is especially well suited to Zones 4–6, 15–17; it also thrives in Zones 7–9 if you substitute locally successful rhododendrons for those listed under E and F on the facing page. To enjoy this patio in Zone 32 as well, again choose rhododendrons that thrive in your climate, and replace the Pacific Coast iris (P) with iris 'Paltec'.

PLANT LIST

A. **Cercis canadensis 'Forest Pansy'.** Eastern redbud (1)

B. **Corylus avellana 'Contorta'.** Harry Lauder's walking stick (1)

C. **Chimonanthus praecox (C. fragrans).** Wintersweet (1)

D. **Acer palmatum 'Ever Red' ('Dissectum Atropurpureum').** Japanese maple (2)

E. **Rhododendron 'Trude Webster'** (2)

F. **Rhododendron 'Unique'** (1)

G. **Pieris japonica 'Mountain Fire'.** Lily-of-the-valley shrub (4)

H. **Pieris japonica 'Variegata'.** Lily-of-the-valley shrub (2)

I. **Rhododendron (azalea) 'Gumpo'** (4)

J. **Mahonia bealei.** Leatherleaf mahonia (2)

K. **Skimmia reevesiana (S. fortunei)** (18)

L. **Actinidia kolomikta** (2)

M. **Clematis 'Henryi'** (2)

N. **Hakonechloa macra 'Aureola'.** Japanese forest grass (8)

O. **Hosta 'Sum and Substance'** (2)

P. **Iris, Pacific Coast native** (5)

Q. **Alchemilla mollis.** Lady's-mantle (6)

R. **Helleborus orientalis.** Lenten rose (10)

S. **Epimedium grandiflorum 'White Queen'.** Bishop's hat (22)

T. **Sagina subulata 'Aurea'.** Scotch moss (3-inch squares, set 6 inches apart)

U. **Pachysandra terminalis 'Silver Edge' ('Variegata').** Japanese spurge (sprigs, set 1 foot apart)

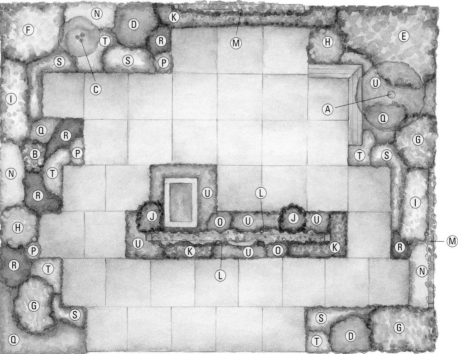

Planting area: 40' x 30'

ALL DECKED OUT

Ready for a long, warm summer, this deck brims with inviting color and enticing fragrances. Its anchor points are the two citrus trees that frame the trellises and provide a leafy, scented backdrop for the seating. In Zones 14–24, where these plants succeed (provided the angel's trumpet is protected from freezes in Zones 14 and 15), bloom begins in midspring and continues into fall. Long-flowering perennials are featured, and assorted annuals intensify the color. Further color notes come from non-green foliage on New Zealand flax, lily turf, heuchera, begonia, licorice plant, dusty miller, 'Crystal Palace' lobelia, and assorted succulents.

PLANT LIST

A. **Citrus (lemon or orange)** (2)
AS UNDERPLANTING: **Lobularia maritima, white** (sweet alyssum)

B. **Brugmansia candida.** Angel's trumpet (1)
AS UNDERPLANTING: **Gazania hybrid, cream; Helichrysum petiolare 'Limelight'** (licorice plant)

C. **Abutilon megapotamicum.** Flowering maple (2, on trellises)
AS UNDERPLANTING: **Begonia (bedding type, bronze leaves); Liriope muscari 'Silvery Sunproof' (big blue lily turf); Campanula poscharskyana** (Serbian bellflower)

D. **Buxus microphylla japonica.** Japanese boxwood (15)

E. **Phormium 'Maori Maiden'.** New Zealand flax (1)
AS UNDERPLANTING: **Petunia × hybrida, pink; Centaurea cineraria (dusty miller); Helichrysum petiolare** (licorice plant)

F. **Heliotropium arborescens (H. peruvianum).** Common heliotrope (3)
AS UNDERPLANTING: **Brachycome multifida** (Swan River daisy); **Verbena × hybrida, white**

G. **Agapanthus 'Peter Pan'.** Lily-of-the-Nile (1)
AS UNDERPLANTING: **Nierembergia hippomanica violacea 'Mont Blanc'** (dwarf cup flower); **Lobelia erinus 'Crystal Palace'**

H. **Hemerocallis 'Stella de Oro'.** Daylily (2)
AS UNDERPLANTING: **Lobelia erinus, white**

I. **Heuchera 'Palace Purple'** (4)

J. **Echeveria imbricata** (hen and chicks) (1); **Sedum sieboldii (Hylotelephium sieboldii)** (1); **Sempervivum, bronze cultivar** (houseleek) (2)

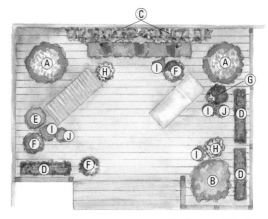

Planting area: 20' x 15'

A SHADY RETREAT

Cool and leafy, this deck is a serene oasis, a perfect place for just relaxing. Thanks to shade from house walls and off-deck trees, it's ideal for deckscaping with favorite shade plants. Unlike the sunny, mass-of-color plan shown opposite, this one gives you flower color in individual bursts off and on from winter through summer. But colorful and variegated foliage does offer a display throughout the growing season: coleus in a rainbow of hues, non-green foliage on hosta, dead nettle, bishop's weed, and heuchera. Try this plan in Zones 4–9, 14–21, being sure to move the potted fuchsia to a sheltered, frost-free spot during winter.

Planting area: 22' x 16'

PLANT LIST

A. **Acer palmatum 'Bloodgood'.** Japanese maple (1)
AS UNDERPLANTING: **Lamium maculatum 'White Nancy'** (dead nettle)

B. **Camellia japonica 'Nuccio's Pearl'** (1)
AS UNDERPLANTING: **Campanula poscharskyana** (Serbian bellflower)

C. **Hydrangea macrophylla, French hybrid.** Bigleaf hydrangea (1)

D. **Rhododendron (azalea) 'Sherwood Pink'** (1)

E. **Aegopodium podagraria.** Bishop's weed (4)

F. **Impatiens wallerana** (9)

G. **Hosta 'Gold Edger'** (4)

H. **Fuchsia 'Gartenmeister Bonstedt'** (1)

I. **Heuchera 'Pewter Veil'** (1)

J. **Hosta sieboldiana 'Elegans'** (2)

K. **Coleus × hybridus** (6)

L. All pots on slat bench are bonsai specimens

PLANT LIST

A. **Lonicera × heckrottii.**
   Gold flame honeysuckle (4)
B. **Ribes sanguineum.** Pink winter currant (1)
C. **Digitalis × mertonensis.** Foxglove (7)
D. **Iris foetidissima.** Gladwin iris (3)
E. **Liriope muscari 'Silvery Sunproof'.**
   Big blue lily turf (6)
F. **Polystichum polyblepharum.**
   Japanese lace fern (2)
G. **Bergenia cordifolia.**
   Heartleaf bergenia (5)
H. **× Heucherella tiarelloides**
   'Bridget Bloom' (6)
I. **Corydalis lutea** (6)
J. **Lamium maculatum 'White Nancy'.**
   Dead nettle (8)
K. **Campanula poscharskyana.**
   Serbian bellflower (7+)
L. **Ajuga reptans.** Carpet bugle (8)
M. **Sagina subulata 'Aurea'.**
   Scotch moss (about twenty-two
   3-inch squares, set 6 inches apart)

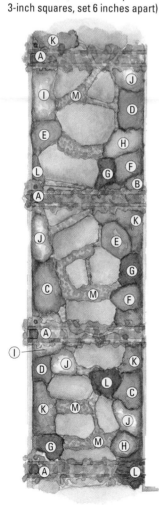

Planting area: 8' x 30'

DOWN THE GARDEN PATH

All too often, the narrow strip between side house wall and property line is ignored, left to serve as a drab conduit between front and back yards. But if you choose your plants carefully, there's no reason you can't include this no-man's-land in the grander scheme of your garden. Here, a stone path leads through an inviting bower. Fragrant honeysuckle on the overheads gives a sense of enclosure, while various low-growing plants and ground covers provide a patchwork carpet of leaf and flower color, punctuated here and there by the vertical accents of foxglove and gladwin iris. Zones 4–9, 14–24, and 32 are congenial climates for this plan; color reaches its peak in spring.

PASSAGEWAY GARDEN

Even a formal, essentially straight path offers an opportunity to transform a forgotten side yard into a passageway garden, with plantings that give you a reason to slow down and admire the view. The lively assortment shown here thrives in day-long dappled sun or light shade, or in a situation where sunny mornings are followed by light shade in the afternoon. Summer bloom time brings the brightest display, but you'll also enjoy more subtle color throughout the growing season from variegated and non-green foliage. This plan does best in Zones 3–6, 32–35, 37, 39–41.

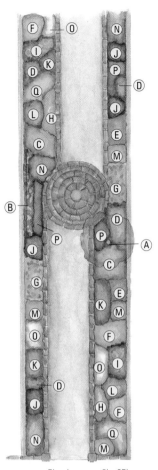

Planting area: 8' x 35'

PLANT LIST

A. Amelanchier × grandiflora. Apple serviceberry (1)

B. Clematis 'Hagley Hybrid' (1)

C. Alchemilla mollis. Lady's-mantle (4)

D. Polygonatum odoratum 'Variegatum'. Solomon's seal (6)

E. Astrantia major. Masterwort (3)

F. Astilbe × arendsii 'Peach Blossom' (4+)

G. Astilbe simplicifolia 'Sprite' (6)

H. Athyrium nipponicum 'Pictum' (A. goeringianum 'Pictum'). Japanese painted fern (5)

I. Brunnera macrophylla 'Variegata' (4)

J. Heuchera 'Pewter Veil' (4)

K. Corydalis flexuosa 'Blue Panda' (6)

L. Hosta 'Frances Williams' (2)

M. Hosta 'Shade Fanfare' (4)

N. Hosta 'Hadspen Blue' (9+)

O. Pulmonaria saccharata 'Mrs. Moon'. Bethlehem sage (6+)

P. Campanula portenschlagiana (C. muralis). Dalmatian bellflower (6)

Q. Hakonechloa macra 'Aureola'. Japanese forest grass (4)

Agapanthus orientalis

ROADSIDE RIOT

In many suburbs, city planners incorporate parking strips into street design—and indeed, these zones between street and sidewalk offer a great gardening opportunity that homeowners too often waste on lawn. Despite their narrowness (widths vary from 3 to about 6 feet), the plots can pack in a dazzling variety of colorful plants, affording both you and passersby great pleasure. What you need are tough plants and, in much of the country, a rudimentary watering system: sandwiched between strips of pavement, these areas can dry out rapidly. In the planting shown here (ideal for Zones 14–24), a kaleidoscope of California favorites sizzles with color from spring through summer.

PLANT LIST

A. **Agapanthus orientalis.**
Lily-of-the-Nile (4)

B. **Phormium 'Yellow Wave'.**
New Zealand flax (1)

C. **Hemerocallis, cream cultivar.**
Daylily (4)

D. **Pennisetum setaceum 'Burgundy Blaze' ('Rubrum Dwarf').**
Fountain grass (3)

E. **Erigeron karvinskianus.**
Mexican daisy,
Santa Barbara daisy (2)

F. **Convolvulus cneorum.**
Bush morning glory (2)

G. **Aloe saponaria** (4)

H. **Echeveria imbricata.**
Hen and chicks (5)

I. **Osteospermum fruticosum.**
Trailing African daisy (6)

J. **Oenothera speciosa (O. berlandieri).**
Mexican evening primrose (5)

K. **Verbena tenuisecta 'Tapien Purple'.**
Moss verbena (8)

L. **Teucrium gussonei (T. cossonii, T. majoricum).** Germander (4)

M. **Cerastium tomentosum.**
Snow-in-summer (11)

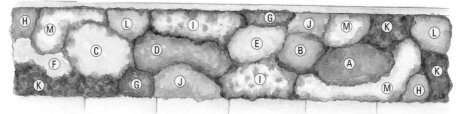

Planting area: 30' x 5½'

Traffic Stopper

Knockout color guaranteed! Blazing in hot hues (with a tempering touch of cool blue and purple), these plants are rugged customers, well suited to life on the street. They're impressively tolerant of varied climates too, thriving in Zones 3–9, 14–17, and 29–41—areas that encompass virtually the entire spectrum of summer and winter conditions. From late spring until autumn, you can count on an arresting show of colorful flowers, with the lamb's ears and fescue providing colored foliage as well. Aside from the shrubby blue mist, all the plants are perennials that need just an annual cleanup (in late fall or early spring, depending on climate) to stay tidy.

TOP: *Gaillardia × grandiflora* 'Goblin'
BOTTOM: *Hemerocallis* 'Stella de Oro'

PLANT LIST

A. **Caryopteris × clandonensis.** Blue mist (2)

B. **Asclepias tuberosa.** Butterfly weed (1)

C. **Liatris spicata 'Kobold'.** Gayfeather (4)

D. **Sedum 'Autumn Joy' (Hylotelephium 'Autumn Joy')** (2)

E. **Festuca 'Elijah Blue'.** Blue fescue (9)

F. **Gaillardia × grandiflora 'Goblin'.** Blanket flower (10)

G. **Hemerocallis 'Stella de Oro'.** Daylily (7)

H. **Achillea tomentosa.** Woolly yarrow (10)

I. **Salvia × superba 'May Night'** (14)

J. **Iberis sempervirens 'Snowflake'.** Evergreen candytuft (5)

K. **Stachys byzantina 'Silver Carpet'.** Lamb's ears (7)

Planting area: 30' x 5½'

Have you ever promised yourself a rose garden? Perhaps you've been yearning for a flower bed that can fill the house with summer bouquets, or for a garden all in white. This

SPECIALTY PLANTINGS

chapter can help you bring those dreams—and many more—to life. We start with "theme" ideas, from plans that showcase the beauties of one season to riotous cottage gardens to designs centered on pools (whether natural or made by the gardener). You'll find a trio of rose gardens, too: one modest, one grand, and one featuring heritage roses.

The next 15 designs are plantings with a purpose. Some are intended to provide flowers for cutting, others herbs for the kitchen; still others are filled with plants chosen for their fragrances. And gardeners who feel that no planting is complete without frequent attention from birds and butterflies won't be disappointed: we've designed five plans to attract just these visitors.

Finally, you'll find color-focused plantings—sizzling-hot combinations, vibrant or muted mixed colors, gray and cool-color plantings, white gardens, and two designs that derive color from foliage alone.

In riotous bloom from spring through summer, this assortment of cottage-garden perennials is a living outdoor bouquet that provides plenty of flowers for cutting, too. Design by Dariel Alexander.

THEMES AND VARIATIONS

Often, we design our gardens with a particular vision in mind: a glorious sweep of spring flowers, a rose plot lush with color and scent, a collection of water lovers to enhance a still backyard pool. If you have only a small space at your disposal, you know you'll have to be very selective in your choices; if your property is larger, you can let yourself go, adopting the motto "nothing succeeds like excess"! The plans on these 18 pages, varying in scale from modest to grand, address a number of themes: seasonal flowers, rose beds, cottage and mixed plantings, water gardens, and—for the ultimate in permanence—shrub collections.

SPRING SYMPHONY

As winter's drear slowly gives way to brighter days, nothing is more heartening than flowers. They first appear in scattered bursts, but as the season progresses, the garden is flooded in waves of bloom. The cheerful assortment of perennials shown here captures all the color and bounty of spring in one compact planting. Some of these plants continue their show into summer or at least offer briefer moments of color later in the year. You'll have the best results with this plan in climates offering some winter chill (Zones 3–9, 14–16, 33, and 34). However, you can also employ it in Zones 2, 35–41 if you make a few substitutions: in place of red-hot poker (A in the list below), use three plants of foxtail lily (*Eremurus,* Shelford hybrids); for gaura (K), substitute three *Penstemon digitalis* 'Husker Red'; for *Geranium* 'Johnson's Blue' (L), use *G. pratense.*

PLANT LIST

A. Kniphofia uvaria, yellow cultivar. Red-hot poker (1)

B. Baptisia australis. Blue false indigo (1)

C. Paeonia 'Festiva Maxima'. Peony (2)

D. Centranthus ruber 'Albus'. Jupiter's beard (4)

E. Penstemon barbatus 'Pink Beauty' (3)

F. Aster × frikartii 'Mönch' (4)

G. Chrysanthemum coccineum (Tanacetum coccineum, Pyrethrum roseum). Pyrethrum, painted daisy (3)

H. Iris, Siberian, 'Caesar's Brother' (1)

I. Hemerocallis, cream cultivar. Daylily (2)

J. Hemerocallis 'Stella de Oro'. Daylily (4)

K. Gaura lindheimeri 'Siskiyou Pink' (1)

L. Geranium 'Johnson's Blue' (4)

M. Papaver orientale, pink cultivar. Oriental poppy (1)

N. Geum chiloense 'Lady Stratheden' (2)

O. Heuchera 'Palace Purple' (6)

P. Iberis sempervirens 'Snowflake'. Evergreen candytuft (2)

Q. Campanula portenschlagiana (C. muralis). Dalmatian bellflower (2)

R. Aurinia saxatilis (Alyssum saxatile). Basket-of-gold (3)

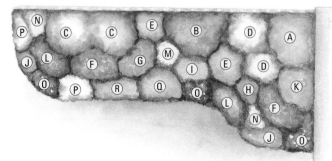

Planting area: 20' x 8'

SUMMER SPLENDOR

Spring may usher in the flowering year, but summer's show is no less dazzling. In fact, many summer-blooming perennials mount a longer-lasting display than spring bloomers do, staying showy throughout the summer and even into autumn. In keeping with the season's temperatures, many of these perennials offer distinctly warm colors. In the plan illustrated here, summery hues of yellow and rosy red are balanced with plenty of white and blue, cool shades that offer welcome (if only psychological!) relief on scorching days. These plants are suited to a wide range of climates: Zones 2–9, 14–17, 32–43.

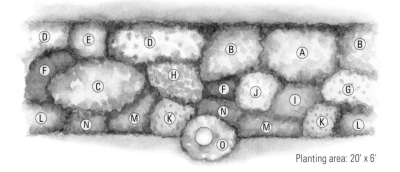

Planting area: 20' x 6'

PLANT LIST

A. **Dictamnus albus 'Albiflorus'.** Gas plant (2)

B. **Achillea millefolium, Summer Pastels strain.** Common yarrow (3+)

C. **Achillea 'Moonshine'** (4)

D. **Echinacea purpurea 'White Swan'** (7+)

E. **Artemisia lactiflora.** White mugwort (1)

F. **Liatris spicata 'Kobold'.** Gayfeather (4)

G. **Chrysanthemum × superbum 'Aglaia'** **(Leucanthemum maximum 'Aglaia').** Shasta daisy (5+)

H. **Limonium latifolium.** Sea lavender (3)

I. **Hemerocallis, cream cultivar.** Daylily (2)

J. **Coreopsis verticillata 'Moonbeam'.** Threadleaf coreopsis (1)

K. **Coreopsis auriculata 'Nana'** (3)

L. **Veronica 'Goodness Grows'** (4+)

M. **Verbena canadensis 'Homestead Purple'** (4)

N. **Potentilla nepalensis 'Miss Willmott' ('Willmottiae').** Cinquefoil (4)

O. **Cerastium tomentosum.** Snow-in-summer (7)

Rudbeckia fulgida sullivantii 'Goldsturm'

A BACKYARD PRAIRIE

You don't have to live in the Midwest to enjoy a view of the prairie out your window: this backyard planting evokes the spirit of the plains, of sweeps of tall grass dotted with native daisies. It's less uniform in appearance than a true prairie, though, with a variety of grasses and perennial flowers set out in discrete drifts—it's a garden, not a recreated meadow. Flower color reaches its peak in summer. Count on these plants for toughness and relatively trouble-free performance in Zones 4–9, 14–17, 32–34. If you replace the feather grass (C in the list below) with purple moor grass *(Molinia caerulea arundinacea* 'Skyracer'), the plan will also succeed in Zones 3, 35, 37, and 39.

PLANT LIST

A. **Miscanthus sinensis 'Morning Light'.** Eulalia grass (1)

B. **Calamagrostis × acutiflora 'Karl Foerster' ('Stricta').** Feather reed grass (1)

C. **Stipa gigantea.** Feather grass (2)

D. **Molinia caerulea.** Purple moor grass (2)

E. **Helictotrichon sempervirens (Avena sempervirens).** Blue oat grass (5)

F. **Pennisetum alopecuroides 'Hameln'.** Fountain grass (5)

G. **Festuca 'Elijah Blue'.** Blue fescue (8)

H. **Perovskia atriplicifolia.** Russian sage (1)

I. **Rudbeckia fulgida sullivantii 'Goldsturm'.** Black-eyed Susan (5)

J. **Echinacea purpurea 'White Swan'** (3)

K. **Liatris spicata 'Silvertips'.** Gayfeather (3)

L. **Achillea filipendulina 'Coronation Gold'.** Fernleaf yarrow (4)

M. **Achillea millefolium, Galaxy strain.** Common yarrow (5)

N. **Achillea 'Moonshine'** (5)

O. **Gaillardia × grandiflora 'Goblin'.** Blanket flower (6)

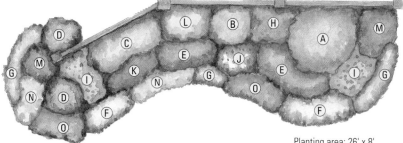

Planting area: 26' x 8'

HARVEST BOUNTY

Autumn clearly signals the close of the gardening year—but it's a terrific last act, brimming with color. Most of the flowering plants in this plan hold their fire through spring and summer, bursting into bloom only when the shorter, crisper days of fall arrive and deciduous trees and shrubs, too, display their year-end finery. The ornamental grasses vary their looks with the seasons, presenting here their last change of costume for the year. Try this plan as an autumn pick-me-up in Zones 3–21, 31–35, 37, 39. To enjoy it in Zones 2, 36, 38, 40, and 41 as well, substitute purple moor grass (*Molinia caerulea*) for the fountain grass (B in the list below).

Heliopsis helianthoides

PLANT LIST

A. Calamagrostis × acutiflora 'Karl Foerster' ('Stricta'). Feather reed grass (3)

B. Pennisetum alopecuroides. Fountain grass (2)

C. Helictotrichon sempervirens (Avena sempervirens). Blue oat grass (2)

D. Boltonia asteroides 'Snowbank' (4)

E. Heliopsis helianthoides 'Golden Plume' (H. scabra 'Golden Plume'). Ox-eye (4)

F. Solidago virgaurea 'Goldenmosa'. Goldenrod (3)

G. Aster novi-belgii 'Audrey'. New York aster (2)

H. Aster novi-belgii 'Marie Ballard'. New York aster (2)

I. Helenium autumnale 'Brilliant'. Common sneezeweed (2)

J. Hemerocallis 'Parian China'. Daylily (2)

K. Sedum 'Autumn Joy' (Hylotelephium 'Autumn Joy') (5)

L. Chrysanthemum pacificum (Dendranthema pacificum). Gold and silver chrysanthemum (2)

M. Chrysanthemum arcticum (Arctanthemum arcticum) (3)

N. Chrysanthemum × morifolium (Dendranthema grandiflorum), cream or light yellow cushion type. Florists' chrysanthemum (7)

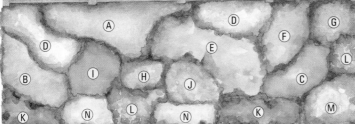

Planting area: 20' x 7'

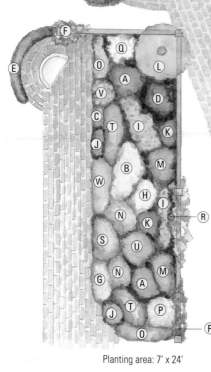

Planting area: 7' x 24'

THREE-SEASON MIXED GARDEN

From spring through fall, this garden's wrought-iron bench offers a prime vantage point for admiring the shifting colors of perennials, shrubs, and graceful crape myrtle. The illustration shows the planting in its early-summer dress, when the rockcress, daylily, cottage pink, and iris have already finished their bloom and the sedum and crape myrtle have yet to flower. Throughout the three growing seasons, you'll enjoy consistent non-green foliage color from the barberry, 'Moonshine' yarrow, lavender, sedum, 'Lime-mound' spiraea, and lamb's ears. This pleasant potpourri is available to gardeners in Zones 7–9, 14, 31.

PLANT LIST

A. Achillea millefolium, Galaxy strain, pink selection. Common yarrow (2)

B. Achillea 'Moonshine' (2)

C. Arabis caucasica (A. albida). Wall rockcress (1)

D. Berberis thunbergii 'Atropurpurea'. Red-leaf Japanese barberry (1)

E. Buxus microphylla koreana. Korean boxwood (8)

F. Clematis 'Henryi' (2)

G. Dianthus plumarius. Cottage pink (3)

H. Baptisia alba. White false indigo (1)

I. Echinacea purpurea. Purple coneflower (9)

J. Hemerocallis 'Little Grapette'. Daylily (5)

K. Iris, Siberian, 'Caesar's Brother' (6)

L. Lagerstroemia indica, pink cultivar. Crape myrtle (1)

M. Lavandula angustifolia. English lavender (3)

N. Liatris spicata 'Kobold'. Gayfeather (4)

O. Nepeta × faassenii. Catmint (5)

P. Rosa 'Heritage' (1)

Q. Rosa 'White Pet' (1)

R. Rosa 'New Dawn' (1)

S. Salvia × superba 'May Night' (4)

T. Sedum 'Autumn Joy' (Hylotelephium 'Autumn Joy') (7)

U. Spiraea × bumalda 'Limemound' (1)

V. Spiraea japonica 'Little Princess' (1)

W. Stachys byzantina 'Silver Carpet'. Lamb's ears (4)

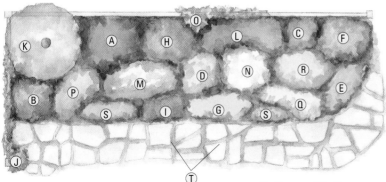

LOW-MAINTENANCE MIXED PLANTING

Unique to this three-season planting is its composition: all the plants are shrubby, from shrubby perennials through true shrubs to a magnolia that blurs the boundary between shrub and tree. The flowering year begins with the magnolia's waxy purple-and-white blossoms, then carries on with the springtime assortment of bloom shown here. Roses, cinquefoil, butterfly bush, blue mist, and dwarf plumbago sustain the show through summer and into early fall. And throughout the seasons, you'll have constant foliage interest from leaves in shades of yellow, bronze, and soft gray. Try this combination in Zones 4–6, 14–17, 32, 34.

Planting area: 24' x 8'

PLANT LIST

A. **Abelia × grandiflora 'Sherwoodii'.** Glossy abelia (1)

B. **Berberis thunbergii 'Cherry Bomb'.** Japanese barberry (1)

C. **Buddleia davidii 'Black Knight'.** Butterfly bush (1)

D. **Caryopteris × clandonensis 'Worcester Gold'.** Blue mist (1)

E. **Ceratostigma plumbaginoides.** Dwarf plumbago (3)

F. **Erysimum 'Bowles Mauve'** (1)

G. **Genista lydia.** Broom (2)

H. **Lavandula angustifolia.** English lavender (3)

I. **Lavandula angustifolia 'Munstead'.** English lavender (2)

J. **Lonicera × heckrottii.** Gold flame honeysuckle (1)

K. **Magnolia 'Randy'** (1)

L. **Nandina domestica 'Woods Dwarf'.** Heavenly bamboo (3)

M. **Potentilla 'Katherine Dykes'.** Cinquefoil (2)

N. **Rosa 'Fair Bianca'** (1)

O. **Rosa 'New Dawn'** (1)

P. **Salvia officinalis 'Berggarten'.** Common sage (2)

Q. **Santolina chamaecyparissus 'Nana'.** Lavender cotton (3)

R. **Spiraea × bumalda 'Limemound'** (2)

S. **Teucrium chamaedrys 'Prostratum'.** Germander (5)

T. **Thymus pseudolanuginosus (T. lanuginosus).** Woolly thyme (between paving stones)

COMPLEAT COTTAGE GARDEN

Even if you don't have a 19th-century cottage, you can still have the garden that would go with it! The essence of such gardens is informality and apparent lack of plan; they give the impression of growing not by design, but simply according to the gardener's changing whims. The original cottage gardens contained just one representative of many different plants, and cottagers even mixed flowers with vegetables to create plantings that were practical as well as aesthetically pleasing. This contemporary homage to the cottage garden (best suited to Zones 4–7, 14, 34, 39) excludes the edibles, but it has all the other traditional characteristics: color, immense variety, and seemingly haphazard design. To adapt the plan to Zones 3, 35–38, 40, and 41, simply replace the lavender (F in the list below) with blue mist (*Caryopteris × clandonensis* 'Dark Knight' or 'Longwood Blue').

PLANT LIST

A. Rosa 'Cornelia' (1)

B. Rosa 'Ballerina' (1)

C. Rosa 'Iceberg' (1)

D. Syringa vulgaris 'President Lincoln'. Common lilac (1)

E. Spiraea × bumalda 'Anthony Waterer' (2)

F. Lavandula angustifolia. English lavender (4)

G. Paeonia 'Festiva Maxima'. Peony (3)

H. Gypsophila paniculata 'Perfecta'. Baby's breath (3)

I. Foeniculum vulgare 'Purpurascens' ('Smokey'). Bronze fennel (1)

J. Alcea rosea (Althaea rosea), Chater's Double strain. Hollyhock (3)

K. Delphinium elatum 'Summer Skies'. Candle delphinium (7)

L. Lupinus, Russell Hybrids. Russell lupine (3)

M. Achillea filipendulina 'Coronation Gold'. Fernleaf yarrow (5)

N. Chrysanthemum × superbum 'Alaska' (Leucanthemum maximum 'Alaska'). Shasta daisy (6)

O. Campanula persicifolia 'Telham Beauty'. Peach-leafed bluebell (5)

P. Aster × frikartii 'Mönch' (6)

Q. Iris, tall bearded, light yellow cultivar (7)

R. Geranium × oxonianum 'Claridge Druce' (4)

S. Scabiosa caucasica. Pincushion flower (6)

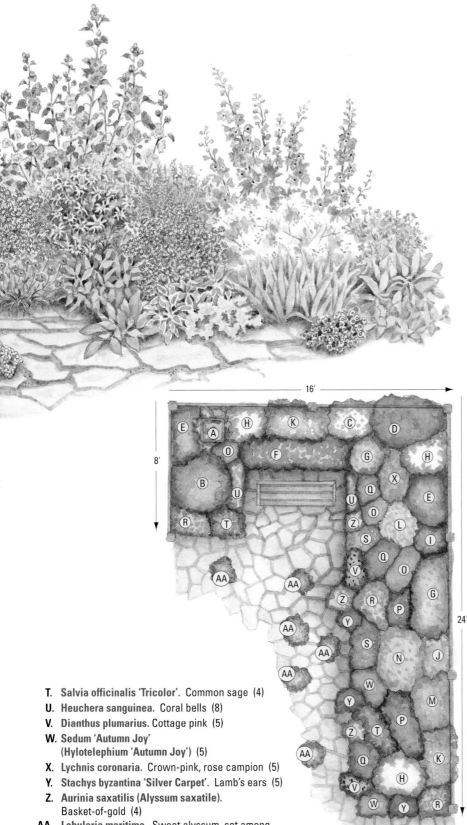

T. **Salvia officinalis 'Tricolor'.** Common sage (4)

U. **Heuchera sanguinea.** Coral bells (8)

V. **Dianthus plumarius.** Cottage pink (5)

W. **Sedum 'Autumn Joy'** **(Hylotelephium 'Autumn Joy')** (5)

X. **Lychnis coronaria.** Crown-pink, rose campion (5)

Y. **Stachys byzantina 'Silver Carpet'.** Lamb's ears (5)

Z. **Aurinia saxatilis (Alyssum saxatile).** Basket-of-gold (4)

AA. **Lobularia maritima.** Sweet alyssum, set among pavers (12)

TOP: *Rosa* 'Ballerina'
CENTER: *Lupinus,* Russsell Hybrids
BOTTOM: *Rosa* 'Iceberg'

COTTAGE CORNER

Soft, fragrant, and colored in whites, creams, pinks, and blues—this is a cottage garden for fairy tales and romances. Many of the plants are frothy, billowy, and filmy, spilling into one another and onto the pavement, but the spikes of delphinium, foxglove, and campanula provide sharp vertical punctuation. Late spring and early summer find the garden at the zenith of its bloom, but the climbing rose, yarrow, delphinium, queen of the prairie, baby's breath, and bee balm continue to provide color later into the year. Zones 4–9, 14–16, and 32 suit all the plants listed; the plan will also succeed in Zones 34 and 39 if you substitute deep pink *Rosa* 'William Baffin' for 'Climbing Cécile Brunner' (M in the list at left).

PLANT LIST

A. **Achillea ptarmica 'The Pearl'** (9)

B. **Campanula glomerata, Alba strain** (6)

C. **Convallaria majalis.**
Lily-of-the-valley (12)

D. **Delphinium elatum 'Summer Skies' and 'Galahad'.** Candle delphinium (9)

E. **Digitalis purpurea, Excelsior strain.**
Common foxglove (7)

F. **Filipendula rubra 'Venusta'.**
Queen of the prairie (5)

G. **Gypsophila paniculata 'Bristol Fairy'.**
Baby's breath (5)

H. **Lavandula angustifolia 'Hidcote'.**
English lavender (6)

I. **Linum perenne.** Perennial blue flax (14)

J. **Monarda didyma 'Croftway Pink'.**
Bee balm (4)

K. **Nigella damascena 'Persian Jewels'.**
Love-in-a-mist (19)

L. **Rosa gallica 'Versicolor' ('Rosa Mundi')** (2)

M. **Rosa 'Climbing Cécile Brunner'** (2)

N. **Viola wittrockiana,**
Imperial Antique Shades strain. Pansy (20)

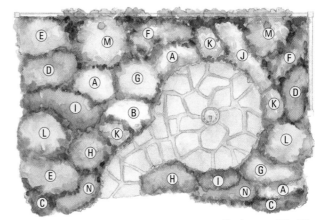

Planting area: 16' x 10'

A GATHERING OF SHRUBS

If you think of shrubs as nothing more than leafy green lumps, useful only for marking property lines, this planting will alter your perception. Leafy they are, but not all are green; and many have showy flowers, while some even bear decorative fruits. The assortment shown here (suited to Zones 3–9, 15–17, 32–35, 37, 39) features flower color off and on from midspring to late summer. Only the arborvitae and juniper are flowerless, but they make up for the lack with year-round color from non-green foliage. The entire scheme works as an island bed, but you can also use it as a boundary planting along a property margin or fence by eliminating the 'Minuet' weigela and the deutzia (L and M in the list at right).

For a planting suited to Zones 36, 38, 40, and 41 as well, replace *Viburnum* 'Eskimo' (B) with either *V. opulus* 'Compactum' or *V. trilobum* 'Compactum'.

PLANT LIST

A. **Viburnum prunifolium.** Black haw (1)

B. **Viburnum 'Eskimo'** (1)

C. **Hydrangea quercifolia 'Snow Queen'.** Oakleaf hydrangea (1)

D. **Philadelphus virginalis 'Glacier'.** Mock orange (1)

E. **Weigela florida 'Variegata'** (3)

F. **Berberis thunbergii 'Atropurpurea'.** Red-leaf Japanese barberry (1)

G. **Thuja occidentalis 'Yellow Ribbon'.** American arborvitae (1)

H. **Spiraea × bumalda 'Anthony Waterer'** (2)

I. **Caryopteris × clandonensis 'Worcester Gold'.** Blue mist (2)

J. **Juniperus sabina 'Blue Danube'.** Savin juniper (2)

K. **Cotoneaster adpressus praecox** (2)

L. **Weigela florida 'Minuet'** (3)

M. **Deutzia gracilis 'Nikko'.** Slender deutzia (2)

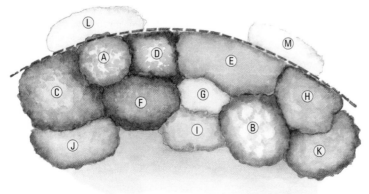

Planting area: 40' x 12' (excluding L and M)

Cistus salviifolius

CALIFORNIA COLLAGE

Abundant sunshine and relatively mild winters make California's Zones 14–24 an ideal climate for an amazing array of plants from around the globe. Those that do best here are also agreeable to one other California characteristic—a long dry period covering most of the growing season. This shrub border is an appropriately unthirsty array; all are flowering plants that reach a crescendo of color in late spring. Another trait they share is foliage in gray to grayish green, a leaf color typical of plants that hail from the world's drier places.

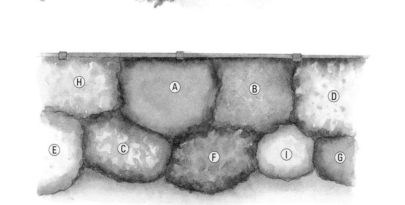

Planting area: 20' x 8'

PLANT LIST

A. **Anisodontea hypomandarum.** Cape mallow (1)

B. **Teucrium fruticans 'Azurea'.** Bush germander (1)

C. **Convolvulus cneorum.** Bush morning glory (2)

D. **Cistus ladanifer.** Crimson-spot rockrose (1+)

E. **Cistus salviifolius.** Sageleaf rockrose (1+)

F. **Cistus 'Warley Rose'.** Rockrose (1)

G. **Lavandula stoechas 'Otto Quast'.** Spanish lavender (1+)

H. **Phlomis fruticosa.** Jerusalem sage (1)

I. **Phlomis lanata** (1)

NOTABLY NORTHWESTERN

In western Washington and Oregon, gardeners consider the plants in this plan virtually foolproof: you plant them, they thrive. Assembled as a shrub border, they present a fetching array of foliage texture and color, as well as striking bursts of flower color from earliest spring well into summer. The Northwest's misty, overcast Zones 4–6 are ideal for these plants, and in these regions they'll take full sun all day. With a bit more attention, they'll succeed in Zones 16, 17, 34, and 37; here, the rhododendrons, lily-of-the-valley shrub, and hydrangea are likely to prefer a little afternoon shade in summer. For a plan suited to Zone 39, replace *Rhododendron* 'Christmas Cheer' (C in the list at right) with *R.* 'Vernus' and substitute *Daphne* × *burkwoodii* 'Carol Mackie' for lily-of-the-valley shrub (E).

PLANT LIST

A. **Magnolia liliiflora (M. quinquepeta).** Lily magnolia (1)

B. **Hydrangea serrata 'Preziosa'** (1)

C. **Rhododendron 'Christmas Cheer'** (1)

D. **Rhododendron (deciduous azalea) 'Irene Koster'** (2)

E. **Pieris japonica 'Variegata'.** Lily-of-the-valley shrub (1)

F. **Kalmia latifolia 'Elf'.** Mountain laurel (1)

G. **Spiraea japonica 'Shirobana' ('Shibori')** (1)

H. **Erica ciliaris 'Stoborough'.** Dorset heath (1+)

I. **Erica vagans 'Lyonesse'.** Cornish heath (1+)

J. **Calluna vulgaris 'Silver King'.** Heather (2)

K. **Calluna vulgaris 'Mrs. Pat'.** Heather (2)

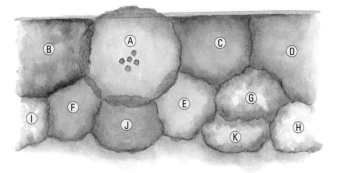

Planting area: 20' x 9'

A ROSY CORNER

So many choices, so little space! For many gardeners, that's the annual lament at bare-root planting time, when nurseries are flooded with roses of all sorts, from brand-new hybrid teas to old-fashioned heritage types. If you have only a modest plot available, make the most of it with this design. Including just 12 different roses, it nonetheless offers the full spectrum of colors in varieties of proven performance and popularity. An assortment of perennials fronts the bed, serving as a colorful, informal transition between the rather stiff rose bushes and the surrounding paving. Zones 4–9, 12–24, and 32 are best for this plan, but you can also use it in Zones 33, 34, and 39 if you give the roses winter protection.

PLANT LIST

- **A.** Rosa 'Climbing Iceberg' (1)
- **B.** Rosa 'Altissimo' (1)
- **C.** Rosa 'Queen Elizabeth' (1)
- **D.** Rosa 'Peace' (1)
- **E.** Rosa 'Fragrant Cloud' (1)
- **F.** Rosa 'Mister Lincoln' (1)
- **G.** Rosa 'Double Delight' (1)
- **H.** Rosa 'Pascali' (1)
- **I.** Rosa 'Perfume Delight' (1)
- **J.** Rosa 'Amber Queen' (1)
- **K.** Rosa 'Europeana' (1)
- **L.** Rosa 'Angel Face' (1)
- **M.** Lavandula angustifolia 'Munstead'. English lavender (5)
- **N.** Geranium himalayense (G. grandiflorum) 'Birch Double' ('Plenum') (2)
- **O.** Geranium cinereum 'Ballerina' (4)
- **P.** Potentilla nepalensis 'Miss Willmott' ('Willmottiae'). Cinquefoil (4)
- **Q.** Dianthus plumarius. Cottage pink (9)
- **R.** Stachys byzantina. Lamb's ears (9)
- **S.** Cerastium tomentosum. Snow-in-summer (6)

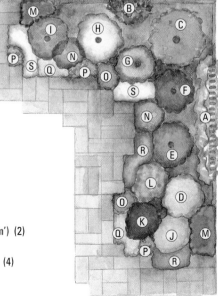

Planting area: 16' x 21'

ROSES IN THE GRAND MANNER

If rosemania strikes and you have the space to indulge it to the full, succumb to your desires with this formal design. It accommodates 51 plants, ranging from climbers to miniatures. The geometric layout, trelliswork, brick paving, and comfortable seating recall estate and park plantings of days gone by—old-fashioned in style, perhaps, but still providing effective display for a sizable rose collection. In maintenance terms, Zones 4–9, 12–24, 30, 32 are best for this planting, but it will also work in Zones 11, 33, 34, and 39 with winter protection for the roses (in Zones 34 and 39, you'll also need to overwinter the potted lily turf in a frost-sheltered spot).

Planting area: 34' x 28'

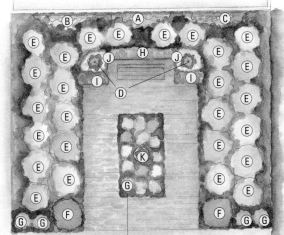

All plants in island are G except as noted.

PLANT LIST

A. Rosa 'New Dawn' (1)

B. Rosa 'Abraham Darby' (1)

C. Rosa 'Graham Thomas' (1)

D. Rosa 'The Fairy', as standard (2)

E. Rosa, hybrid tea (assorted) (26)

F. Rosa, floribunda cultivar (2)

G. Rosa, miniature (assorted) (18)

H. Lavandula × intermedia 'Grosso'. Lavandin (6)

I. Lavandula angustifolia 'Hidcote'. English lavender (8)

J. Artemisia stellerana 'Silver Brocade'. Beach wormwood (14)

K. Liriope muscari 'Majestic'. Big blue lily turf (in urn) (1)

ROSES FROM THE PAST

The roses of yesterday are not outmoded or obsolete. Quite to the contrary, they're being rediscovered, retrieved, and cherished by thousands of gardeners enchanted by the styles and histories of old or "heritage" roses. Unlike most modern hybrid teas, grandifloras, and floribundas, many heritage sorts are informal to lax shrubs that should not be planted in stiff, precisely spaced ranks. Give them room to mound, sprawl, or droop, then

Rosa 'Marie Louise'

enjoy the resulting floral resplendence. This plan features eight old rose types—gallica, damask, alba, moss, China, tea, Noisette, and polyantha—in colors ranging from white and soft yellow to pink shades and deep red. Accompanying the roses are assorted perennials, many of them also suitably antique. Zones 4–9, 14–24 yield the best results; with winter protection of the climbers, Zone 32 is also possible.

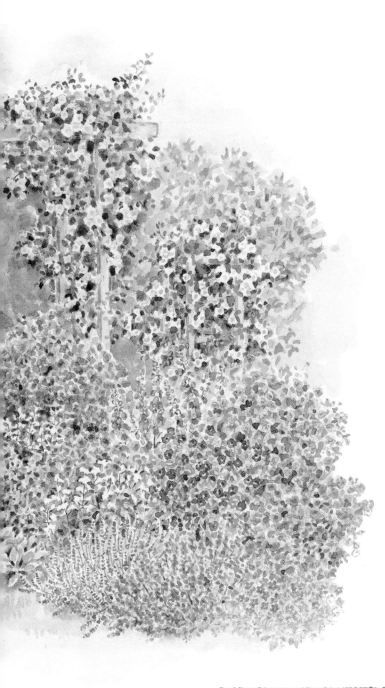

PLANT LIST

A. Rosa 'Awakening' (1)

B. Rosa 'Sombreuil' (1)

C. Rosa 'Alister Stella Gray' (1)

D. Rosa 'Alba Maxima' (1)

E. Rosa 'Great Maiden's Blush' (1)

F. Rosa 'Mme. Lambard' ('Mme. Lombard') (1)

G. Rosa 'Duchesse de Brabant' (1)

H. Rosa 'Marie Louise' (1)

I. Rosa 'Paul Ricault' (1)

J. Rosa 'Alfred de Dalmas' (1)

K. Rosa 'Empress Josephine' (1)

L. Rosa 'Perle d'Or' (1)

M. Rosa 'Hermosa' (1)

N. Rosa 'Comte de Chambord' (1)

O. Rosa 'Superb Tuscan' ('Tuscany Superb') (1)

P. Rosa 'Grüss an Aachen' (1)

Q. Rosa 'Pink Grüss an Aachen' (1)

R. Ilex cornuta 'Dazzler'. Chinese holly (6+)

S. Juniperus chinensis 'Hetz's Columnaris'. Chinese juniper (5)

T. Digitalis purpurea. Common foxglove (10)

U. Lavandula × intermedia 'Provence'. Lavandin (6)

V. Centranthus ruber 'Albus'. Jupiter's beard (7)

W. Geranium pratense. Meadow cranesbill (4)

X. Geranium sanguineum. Bloody cranesbill (4)

Y. Nepeta × faassenii. Catmint (7)

Z. Dianthus plumarius. Cottage pink (8)

AA. Iberis sempervirens 'Snowflake'. Evergreen candytuft (4)

BB. Aurinia saxatilis (Alyssum saxatile) 'Citrina' ('Lutea'). Basket-of-gold (5)

CC. Stachys byzantina 'Silver Carpet'. Lamb's ears (7)

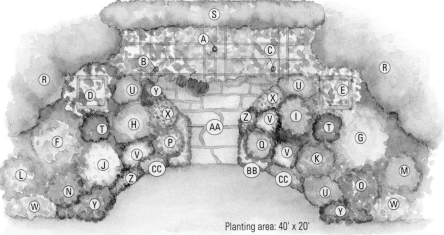

Planting area: 40' x 20'

A SHADED POOL

Soothing shade and tranquil water are sure to ease stress and restore the spirit. No strident colors assault the eye, demanding attention; instead, chartreuse and silvery leaves offer a counterpoint to basic green, while a smattering of pastel blossoms assort with the foliage in subtly attractive combinations. Bloom is most noticeable (though never overwhelming) in spring and summer. This serenity can be yours if you garden in Zones 4–9, 14–17, 32, and 34.

THE PLANTS

A. **Mahonia bealei.** Leatherleaf mahonia (1)

B. **Rhododendron 'Moonstone'** (1)

C. **Alchemilla mollis.** Lady's-mantle (3)

D. **Milium effusum 'Aureum'.** Bowles' golden grass (3)

E. **Hosta 'Gold Edger'** (16)

F. **Lamium maculatum 'White Nancy'.** Dead nettle (18)

G. **× Heucherella tiarelloides 'Pink Frost'** (5)

H. **Athyrium nipponicum 'Pictum' (A. goeringianum 'Pictum').** Japanese painted fern (5)

I. **Sagina subulata.** Irish moss (about sixteen 3-inch squares, set 6 inches apart)

J. **Nymphaea, hardy hybrid.** Water lily (optional) (1)

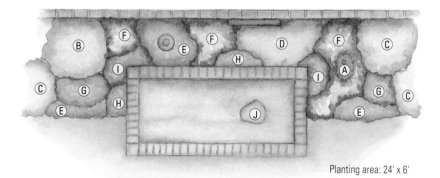

Planting area: 24' x 6'

GONE FISHIN'

You'd almost expect to find fish biting in this naturalistic pond. With luck, you'll have a suitable natural pond to adorn with these moisture-loving plants—but with a little contrivance, you can create your own pool and take the plan from there. Noteworthy is the assortment of foliage types: grasslike in rush and sedge, swordlike in irises and acorus, finely cut and fernlike in goat's beard and astilbe, huge and paddlelike in the ligularia. Flowering runs from spring through early fall, beginning with irises and marsh marigold and finishing with turtlehead, hardy ageratum, and astilbe. Try this plan in Zones 3–7, 15–17, 32, 34, 36–41.

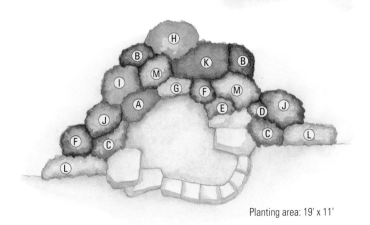

Planting area: 19' x 11'

THE PLANTS

- **A. Iris virginica.** Southern blue flag (3)
- **B. Iris pseudacorus.** Yellow flag (3)
- **C. Carex morrowii expallida (C. m. 'Variegata').** Variegated Japanese sedge (5)
- **D. Juncus effusus.** Soft rush (1)
- **E. Acorus gramineus 'Variegatus'** (2)
- **F. Chelone obliqua.** Turtlehead (3)
- **G. Caltha palustris.** Marsh marigold (2)
- **H. Aruncus dioicus (A. sylvester).** Goat's beard (1)
- **I. Filipendula ulmaria.** Meadow sweet (1)
- **J. Eupatorium coelestinum 'Cori'.** Hardy ageratum (4)
- **K. Astilbe chinensis taquetii 'Purple Lance'** (3)
- **L. Astilbe simplicifolia 'Sprite'** (6)
- **M. Ligularia stenocephala 'The Rocket'** (3)

DESIGNED FOR A PURPOSE

Anyone who plans and plants a garden wants the result to be beautiful. But sometimes the objectives go beyond mere prettiness to include a particular purpose. In the following pages, you'll find plans that focus on some of the "extras" gardeners most often want. For those who love fragrance, there are designs emphasizing scented flowers and foliage. A duo of cut-flower plantings will please those who like to take the garden indoors; a half-dozen plans for herb and kitchen gardens will delight cooks and history buffs alike. And for backyard naturalists, we've devised bird and butterfly gardens certain to deliver abundant seasonal entertainment.

SUMMER ANNUALS FOR CUTTING

Nothing equals annual flowers for abundance and duration of bloom. This flashy patch brings together some of the best cut-flower sorts, along with a single non-annual addition: a clump of shrubby perennial dahlias. A planting of this kind must be taken out when the growing season ends and started from scratch the next year; even the dahlias, though technically perennial tubers, should be lifted and stored over winter. Such yearly replanting does, of course, entail a fair amount of early-season labor—but your work will be rewarded with the garden's later luxuriance, as shown below. In addition, starting fresh each year lets you try out new arrangements, new color schemes, and new plant varieties as the mood strikes. And annuals offer one other undeniable advantage: they'll succeed in all zones.

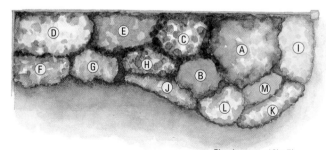

Planting area: 18' x 7'

PLANT LIST

A. Dahlia (2)

B. Moluccella laevis. Bells-of-Ireland (3)

C. Scabiosa atropurpurea. Pincushion flower (4)

D. Cosmos bipinnatus, Sensation strain (6)

E. Consolida ambigua, Steeplechase strain. Larkspur (3)

F. Centaurea cyanus. Cornflower, bachelor's button (6)

G. Antirrhinum majus. Snapdragon (6)

H. Helichrysum bracteatum. Strawflower (6)

I. Tagetes erecta, Sundance strain or other mid-height yellow. African marigold (8)

J. Tagetes patula. French marigold (6)

K. Limonium sinuatum. Sea lavender (6)

L. Zinnia elegans (6)

M. Celosia 'Plumosa'. Plume cockscomb (4)

A PERMANENT CUTTING GARDEN

Annuals don't have a lock on the cut-flower category. Many perennials, too, bloom lavishly enough to be enjoyed indoors as well as in their garden beds. This simple rectangle, measuring just 6 feet across, contains some of the best, most widely adapted cut-flower perennials, all suited to Zones 1–9, 14, 18–21, 32–43. Bloom reaches a peak in summer—but the first flowers appear in spring, and the show doesn't completely close until fall.

Tucked in among the perennial throng is one indispensable "outsider": the hybrid tea rose 'Mister Lincoln'. What is the classic cut flower, after all, if not a long-stemmed red rose?

Because the planting is bounded on three sides by lawn and pavement, access for maintenance is simple. In Zones 1–3, 32–43, this maintenance will include some degree of winter protection for 'Mister Lincoln'.

Planting area: 6' x 17'

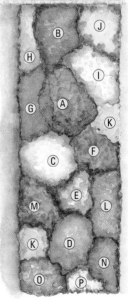

PLANT LIST

A. Rosa 'Mister Lincoln' (1)

B. Adenophora confusa. Lady bells (2)

C. Gypsophila paniculata 'Perfecta'. Baby's breath (1)

D. Phlox paniculata 'Eva Cullum'. Summer phlox (3)

E. Malva alcea 'Fastigiata'. Mallow (2)

F. Penstemon barbatus 'Rose Elf' (3)

G. Aster × frikartii 'Mönch' (3)

H. Chrysanthemum × rubellum 'Clara Curtis' (Dendranthema zawadskii 'Clara Curtis') (3)

I. Chrysanthemum × superbum 'Aglaia' (Leucanthemum maximum 'Aglaia'). Shasta daisy (6)

J. Coreopsis grandiflora 'Sunburst' (5)

K. Sedum 'Autumn Joy' (Hylotelephium 'Autumn Joy') (4)

L. Limonium latifolium. Sea lavender (2)

M. Liatris spicata 'Kobold'. Gayfeather (3)

N. Veronica 'Sunny Border Blue' (3)

O. Scabiosa caucasica. Pincushion flower (3)

P. Dianthus × allwoodii 'Aqua'. Pink (3)

Viola odorata varieties

BREATHE DEEPLY

Step into the garden, take a seat on the strategically placed bench, and inhale! This planting combines over a dozen famously fragrant perennials and shrubs—but you won't have to risk olfactory overload by trying to take in their varied perfumes all at once. Flowering starts with sweet violets in early spring, then progresses to lily-of-the-valley, lilac, mock orange, viburnum, and peony as the season advances. The remaining plants begin their bloom in late spring or early summer; in milder regions, rose and heliotrope will linger into autumn. All these plants should thrive in Zones 2–6, 32–41, though the potted heliotrope will need winter shelter in a frost-free location.

PLANT LIST

A. Syringa vulgaris 'President Lincoln'. Common lilac (1)

B. Viburnum carlesii. Korean spice viburnum (1)

C. Clethra alnifolia. Summersweet (2)

D. Philadelphus virginalis 'Dwarf Minnesota Snowflake'. Mock orange (1)

E. Rosa 'Rotes Meer' ('Purple Pavement') (2)

F. Paeonia 'Edulis Superba'. Peony (2)

G. Dictamnus albus. Gas plant (2)

H. Phlox paniculata 'Eva Cullum'. Summer phlox (4)

I. Hemerocallis lilio-asphodelus (H. flava). Lemon daylily (5)

J. Convallaria majalis. Lily-of-the-valley (7)

K. Viola odorata. Sweet violet (7)

L. Reseda odorata. Mignonette (12)

M. Heliotropium arborescens (H. peruvianum). Common heliotrope (1, in pot)

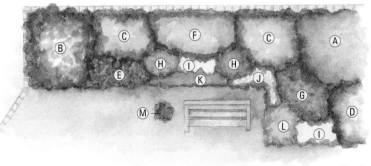

Planting area: 24' x 9'

A SCENTED RETREAT

In milder-winter Zones 9, 14–24, this plan gives gardeners even more to savor than fabulously fragrant flowers. Fully a third of the garden's occupants have leaves that reward a casual pinch or crush with a puff of perfume—lemon, pineapple, anise, mint, and that fragrance in a class of its own: lavender. Shrubs form the backbone of the garden; perennials and one bulb (soft pink, headily sweet amarcrinum) fill out the design. Pockets of two blooming annuals—flowering tobacco and sweet alyssum—complete the bouquet. Vining woodbine adds a double dose of color: its blooms are followed by shiny red berries.

PLANT LIST

A. **Lonicera periclymenum 'Serotina'.** Woodbine (1)

B. **Buddleia davidii 'Black Knight'.** Butterfly bush (1)

C. **Rosa 'Frau Dagmar Hartopp' ('Fru Dagmar Hastrup')** (2)

D. **Aloysia triphylla (Lippia citriodora).** Lemon verbena (1)

E. **Lavandula angustifolia.** English lavender (2)

F. **Lavandula × intermedia 'Grosso'.** Lavandin (7)

G. **Agastache foeniculum.** Anise hyssop (2)

H. **Salvia elegans.** Pineapple sage (2)

I. **Iris, tall bearded, purple cultivar** (2)

J. **× Amarcrinum memoria-corsii (× A. 'Howardii', × Crinodonna memoria-corsii)** (1)

K. **Calamintha nepetoides.** Calamint (3)

L. **Dianthus plumarius.** Cottage pink (6)

M. **Teucrium gussonei (T. cossonii, T. majoricum).** Germander (3)

N. **Nicotiana alata.** Flowering tobacco (4)

O. **Nicotiana alata, Domino strain.** Flowering tobacco (6)

P. **Lobularia maritima.** Sweet alyssum (16)

Q. **Gardenia jasminoides 'White Gem'** (1, in container)

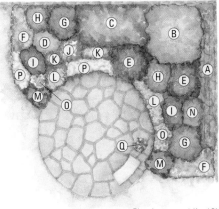

Planting area: 14' x 18'

Chives *(Allium schoenoprasum)*

POCKET-SIZE HERB SAMPLER

Just 48 square feet is space enough for a diverse assortment of scented herbs plus a compatible fragrant rose. Seven of the nine herbs have culinary uses, making this planting especially appealing to cooks (particularly if it's located near a kitchen door). The two nonculinary choices—lavender cotton and catmint—add to the plot's beauty with their soft textures and equally soft gray-green to gray-white leaf color. In fact, much of this garden's charm derives from its varied foliage colors and textures; conspicuous flowers appear chiefly on the chives, catmint, lavender cotton, rosemary, and rose. All the plants will grow in Zones 4–24, 30, 32. In Zone 33, choose the hardy rosemary cultivar 'Arp' for G in the list below.

PLANT LIST

A. **Allium schoenoprasum.** Chives (3)

B. **Artemisia dracunculus.** French tarragon (4)

C. **Nepeta** × **faassenii.** Catmint (3)

D. **Origanum majorana (Majorana hortensis).** Sweet marjoram (1)

E. **Origanum vulgare.** Oregano (2)

F. **Rosa 'Sunsprite'** (1)

G. **Rosmarinus officinalis.** Rosemary (1)

H. **Salvia officinalis 'Icterina'.** Common sage (1)

I. **Santolina chamaecyparissus 'Nana'.** Lavender cotton (3)

J. **Thymus** × **citriodorus 'Aureus'.** Lemon thyme (1)

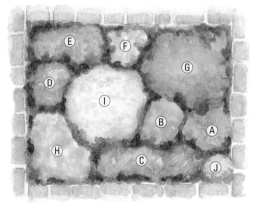

Planting area: 8' x 6'

LINGER AWHILE WITH HERBS

The soothing magic of flowers, fragrance, and appealingly varied foliage textures will lure you to this garden again and again. Offering a potpourri of relaxing, restrained blossom and leaf colors, the herbs in the design include selections used (now or in the past) in medicine and perfumery as well as those of culinary value. The illustration shows the garden in early summer, but bloom time covers a long season, starting in early to midspring and concluding at summer's end. The scented geranium must spend the winter in a sheltered, frost-free location; the other plants succeed outdoors year-round in Zones 4–24, 30, 32–34, 39. To enjoy the plan in Zones 3, 36–38, 40, and 41, replace the two lavenders (B and C in the list below) with anise hyssop (*Agastache foeniculum)* and *Hyssopus officinalis,* respectively.

Achillea 'Moonshine'

PLANT LIST

A. **Rosa gallica 'Officinalis'.** Apothecary's rose (2)

B. **Lavandula angustifolia.** English lavender (2)

C. **Lavandula angustifolia 'Hidcote'.** English lavender (2)

D. **Artemisia absinthium 'Lambrook Silver'.** Common wormwood (2)

E. **Ruta graveolens.** Rue (2)

F. **Salvia officinalis 'Purpurascens'.** Common sage (1)

G. **Salvia officinalis 'Tricolor'.** Common sage (1)

H. **Achillea 'Moonshine'** (4)

I. **Foeniculum vulgare 'Purpurascens'** ('Smokey'). Bronze fennel (1)

J. **Echinacea purpurea.** Purple coneflower (9)

K. **Iris, tall bearded, 'Pallida Variegata'** ('Zebra') (2)

L. **Chrysanthemum parthenium 'Aureum'** (C. p. 'Golden Feather', Tanacetum parthenium 'Aureum'). Feverfew (3)

M. **Dianthus plumarius.** Cottage pink (6)

N. **Nepeta** × **faassenii.** Catmint (2)

O. **Viola odorata.** Sweet violet (2)

P. **Prunella grandiflora.** Self-heal (2)

Q. **Thymus** × **citriodorus.** Lemon thyme (1)

R. **Stachys byzantina.** Lamb's ears (6)

S. **Pelargonium odoratissimum.** Apple geranium (1)

Planting area: 20' x 12'

TIED UP IN KNOTS

Gardeners have enjoyed intricate knot plantings for hundreds of years, delighting in their fanciful yet formal designs. Shown here is the *closed* knot, composed of two or more kinds of plants set out to form an interweaving pattern; the short, dense evergreen herbs historically used for such knots are still ideal for the purpose today. Traditional patterns are many and varied, but the typical knot garden fits within a 12-foot square—as does the planting illustrated directly below, though the circle and arcs of

its design obscure the underlying square frame. Gravel fills the gray areas between the clipped arcs, forming part of the design and also offering easy access to the planting's interior for frequent trimming. The alternate plan at lower left is more obviously square and uses just one more plant, a green-and-gold sage. Try both garden whimsies in Zones 4–24, 29, 30, 32. To extend the plans into Zones 3, 33, 34, and 39, replace *Santolina rosmarinifolia* (B in the list below) with *Hyssopus officinalis.*

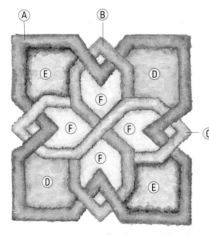

Planting area: 12' x 12'

PLANT LIST

A. Teucrium chamaedrys. Germander (24)

B. Santolina rosmarinifolia (S. virens) (28)

C. Santolina chamaecyparissus. Lavender cotton (28)

D. Calendula officinalis, dwarf strain, yellow. Pot marigold (24)

E. Calendula officinalis, dwarf strain, cream. Pot marigold (24)

F. Salvia officinalis 'Icterina'. Common sage (12; only in alternate plan)

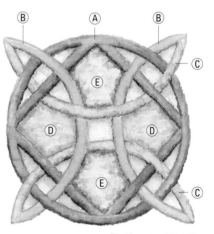

Planting area: 12' x 12'

FORMALITY WITH FLOWERS AND HERBS

The boxwood hedge, symmetrical beds, and sundial recall a formal English garden, but in its choice of plants, this double-bed plan is really a cottage garden with herbs. Oregano, thyme, and sage are the culinary selections; more prominently featured are various herbs traditionally used in medicine and perfumery, interspersed with favorite perennials (peony, daylily, coral bells) and small shrubs (the spiraeas). The plan can shrink or expand:

either bed can stand alone, or you can repeat each one to make a square garden divided by intersecting pathways. You'll have the best success with this planting in Zones 4–9, 14–16, 32–34, 39. To enjoy it in Zones 2, 3, 35–38, 40, and 41 as well, replace C, J, and Y in the list below with (respectively) blue mist *(Caryopteris × clandonensis)*, garden burnet *(Sanguisorba minor)*, and Korean boxwood *(Buxus microphylla koreana)*.

PLANT LIST

A. **Rosa gallica 'Officinalis'.** Apothecary's rose (2)

B. **Spiraea × bumalda 'Limemound'** (1)

C. **Lavandula angustifolia.** English lavender (3)

D. **Ruta graveolens.** Rue (4)

E. **Artemisia absinthium.** Common wormwood (4)

F. **Hyssopus officinalis.** Hyssop (3)

G. **Salvia officinalis 'Purpurascens'.** Common sage (3)

H. **Spiraea × bumalda 'Anthony Waterer'** (2)

I. **Echinacea purpurea.** Purple coneflower (10)

J. **Teucrium chamaedrys.** Germander (7)

K. **Alchemilla mollis.** Lady's-mantle (2)

L. **Thymus × citriodorus 'Argenteus'.** Silver thyme (2)

M. **Thymus × citriodorus 'Aureus'.** Lemon thyme (2)

N. **Dianthus plumarius.** Cottage pink (4)

O. **Paeonia 'Festiva Maxima'.** Peony (2)

P. **Hemerocallis, pink cultivar.** Daylily (4)

Q. **Hemerocallis 'Stella de Oro'.** Daylily (1)

R. **Sedum 'Autumn Joy' (Hylotelephium 'Autumn Joy')** (6)

S. **Chrysanthemum parthenium 'Aureum' (C. p. 'Golden Feather', Tanacetum parthenium 'Aureum').** Feverfew (5)

T. **Iris pallida** (1)

U. **Nepeta × faassenii.** Catmint (3)

V. **Origanum vulgare 'Aureum'.** Oregano (2)

W. **Stachys byzantina 'Silver Carpet'.** Lamb's ears (5)

X. **Heuchera sanguinea.** Coral bells (6)

Y. **Buxus microphylla japonica.** Japanese boxwood (48)

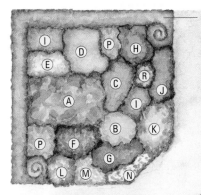

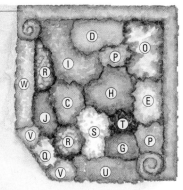

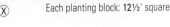

Each planting block: 12½' square

Rhubarb *(Rheum × cultorum)*

MIXED KITCHEN GARDEN

Here's a garden of edibles covering a wide culinary spectrum, from fruits to vegetables to savory herbs. The focal point of the design is the living fence of espaliered dwarf apple trees; brick paths allow easy access for harvest and pruning. The nasturtiums, basil, sweet peppers, and pot marigolds are annuals and must be planted anew each year; the remaining fruits and vegetables are permanent-resident perennials or shrubs that need only some annual maintenance or cleanup. Zones 4–6, 17, 32, 34–41 are favorable regions for this planting; to adapt it to Zones 14–16, 30, 31, and 33, replace the blueberry (C in the list below) with genetic dwarf peach 'Bonanza II'. In Zones 15–17, select an apple cultivar that needs little winter chill.

PLANT LIST

A. **Malus pumila, dwarfed cultivar.** Apple (2)
B. **Asparagus officinalis.** Asparagus (4)
C. **Vaccinium corymbosum.** Blueberry (2)
D. **Calendula officinalis.** Pot marigold (8)
E. **Allium schoenoprasum.** Chives (6)
F. **Monarda didyma 'Cambridge Scarlet'.** Bee balm (2)
G. **Capsicum annuum annuum.** Sweet pepper (5)
H. **Rheum × cultorum.** Rhubarb (2)
I. **Origanum vulgare.** Oregano (2)
J. **Salvia officinalis 'Icterina'.** Common sage (1)
K. **Salvia officinalis 'Purpurascens'.** Common sage (1)
L. **Salvia officinalis 'Tricolor'.** Common sage (1)
M. **Ocimum basilicum 'Dark Opal'.** Sweet basil (6)
N. **Thymus × citriodorus 'Aureus'.** Lemon thyme (4)
O. **Tropaeolum majus.** Garden nasturtium (4)

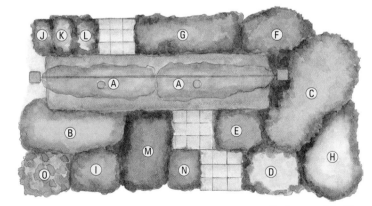

Planting area: 30' x 15'

KITCHEN GARDEN OF HERBS

When a modest cornucopia of culinary herbs grows just a few steps away from the kitchen, it's a simple matter to pop outside and snip a few sprigs to add to the dishes simmering indoors. Besides enhancing your cooking, frequent clipping helps keep the shrubby herbs compact and bushy. In this plan, two favorites get special planting treatment. Spearmint is confined to a large container to keep its invasive tendencies in check. The bay tree, too, is displayed in its own terra-cotta pot, since it needs winter protection in some areas. It's suited to year-round outdoor culture only in Zones 5–9, 14–24; in the other regions to which this scheme is adapted (Zones 4, 10, 11, 30–32), it must overwinter in a frost-free shelter. Gardeners in Zone 33 can also use this plan if they choose the rosemary cultivar 'Arp' for I in the list below. Sweet marjoram (G) will be an annual in Zones 32 and 33; sweet basil (B) is an annual in all zones.

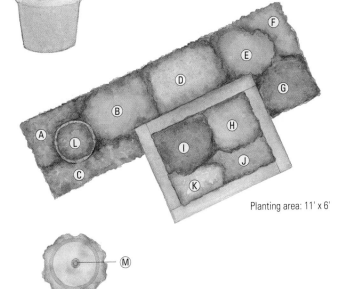

PLANT LIST

A. **Petroselinum crispum.**
Parsley (2)

B. **Ocimum basilicum.** Sweet basil (6)

C. **Allium schoenoprasum.** Chives (8)

D. **Salvia officinalis.** Common sage (2)

E. **Origanum vulgare.** Oregano (2)

F. **Artemisia dracunculus.**
French tarragon (2)

G. **Origanum majorana (Majorana hortensis).** Sweet marjoram (1)

H. **Satureja montana.** Winter savory (2)

I. **Rosmarinus officinalis.** Rosemary (1)

J. **Thymus vulgaris.** Common thyme (1)

K. **Thymus** × **citriodorus 'Aureus'.**
Lemon thyme (1)

L. **Mentha spicata.** Spearmint (2)

M. **Laurus nobilis.** Sweet bay (1)

Planting area: 11' x 6'

TOP: *Echinacea purpurea* with female American goldfinch

CENTER: *Cotoneaster apiculatus*

BOTTOM: *Crataegus phaenopyrum* with male cardinal

CALLING ALL BIRDS

Keep a variety of birds happy throughout the year with this expansive planting. Its varied shrubs and trees offer sites for shelter and nesting—and even a measure of protection, thanks to the thorny stems of barberry and Washington thorn. The food supply is ample, too: many of the plants produce berries from late summer through winter, while the birches, perennials, and moor grass bear an abundance of tasty seeds. Aphids (a bane to gardeners, a favored snack for many birds) are likely to be found on the birches and viburnums. An elevated pool provides a safe place for a drink or a dip.

This plan is suited to larger properties, where it would serve nicely as transition from maintained yard to open field or woods. The plants all need at least some winter chill and do best in Zones 3–6, 31–35, 37, 39. In Zones 36, 38, 40, and 41, replace the doublefile viburnum (D in the plant list) with either *Viburnum opulus* or *V. sargentii*.

PLANT LIST

A. **Betula nigra 'Heritage'.** River birch (3+)

B. **Crataegus phaenopyrum.**
Washington thorn (3)

C. **Juniperus chinensis 'Hetz's Columnaris'.**
Chinese juniper (1)

D. **Viburnum plicatum tomentosum 'Shasta'.**
Doublefile viburnum (1)

E. **Euonymus alata.** Winged euonymus (1)

F. **Amelanchier alnifolia.** Saskatoon (1)

G. **Viburnum opulus 'Compactum'.**
European cranberry bush (1)

H. **Berberis thunbergii 'Atropurpurea'.**
Red-leaf Japanese barberry (2)

I. **Aronia arbutifolia.** Red chokeberry (2)

J. **Cotoneaster adpressus praecox** (3)

K. **Cotoneaster apiculatus.**
Cranberry cotoneaster (2)

L. **Cotoneaster dammeri.**
Bearberry cotoneaster (3)

M. **Echinacea purpurea.**
Purple coneflower (12)

N. **Coreopsis grandiflora 'Sunburst'** (12)

O. **Molinia caerulea.** Purple moor grass (4)

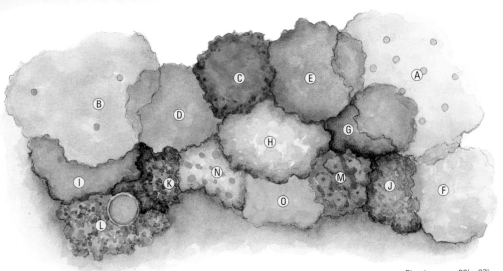

Planting area: 60' x 27'

WESTERN BIRDSCAPE

Smaller than the extensive plan for colder regions shown on pages 88–89, this scaled-down design is suited to mild-winter Zones 8, 9, 12–24. Though it lacks trees and a watering hole, it otherwise offers the same inducements as the larger plan: berries, seeds, and shelter. The irresistible lure—as legions of gardeners have come to know—is the yearly crop of firethorn berries, but the garden's feathered patrons will also feast on the fruits of lantana, heavenly bamboo, cotoneaster, and elaeagnus. Seed-eaters will appreciate the bounty of coreopsis, blanket flower, black-eyed Susan, and fountain grass. The shrubs all afford ample shelter, with the firethorn's forbidding spines providing some protection as well.

PLANT LIST

A. **Elaeagnus × ebbingei** (1)

B. **Pyracantha coccinea 'Kasan'.** Firethorn (1)

C. **Lantana 'Radiation'** (3+)

D. **Nandina domestica.** Heavenly bamboo (2)

E. **Cotoneaster salicifolius 'Emerald Carpet'.**
Willowleaf cotoneaster (2+)

F. **Rudbeckia fulgida sullivantii 'Goldsturm'.**
Black-eyed Susan (11)

G. **Pennisetum setaceum.** Fountain grass (6)

H. **Gaillardia × grandiflora.** Blanket flower (5)

I. **Coreopsis grandiflora 'Sunburst'** (4)

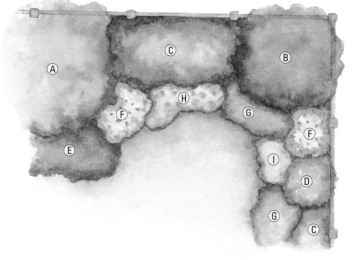

Planting area: 25' x 18'

HUMMINGBIRD CORNER

This colorful garden nook offers long-lasting floral bounty: a feast for the gardener's eyes, a literal banquet for hummingbirds. The blossoms feature the birds' favorite vivid reds and blues, and all provide plentiful, readily available nectar that makes any flight worth the effort. The tantalizing tableau lures hummers over a prolonged period, beginning in mid- or late spring and continuing through summer (and even into fall, in mild-winter areas). The plants listed here will thrive over much of good hummingbird territory: Zones 2–9, 14–17, 32–41. Note that the three annuals—flowering tobacco, scarlet sage, and petunia—will require replanting each year.

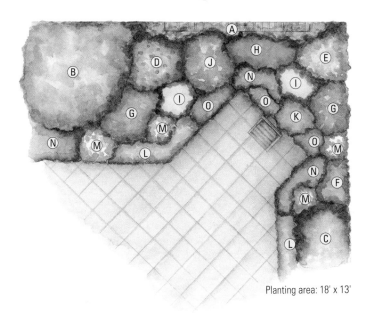

Planting area: 18' x 13'

PLANT LIST

A. Lonicera periclymenum 'Serotina'. Woodbine (1)

B. Weigela florida 'Bristol Ruby' (1)

C. Weigela florida 'Minuet' (1)

D. Monarda didyma 'Jacob Cline'. Bee balm (6)

E. Alcea rosea (Althaea rosea). Hollyhock (7)

F. Digitalis × mertonensis. Foxglove (4)

G. Agastache foeniculum. Anise hyssop (9)

H. Penstemon barbatus 'Prairie Fire' (4)

I. Asclepias tuberosa, yellow cultivar. Butterfly weed (3)

J. Salvia × superba 'Blue Hill' (6)

K. Lychnis chalcedonica. Maltese cross (4)

L. Heuchera sanguinea. Coral bells (9+)

M. Nicotiana alata, Nicki strain, mixed colors. Flowering tobacco (12)

N. Salvia splendens, dwarf red strain. Scarlet sage (16)

O. Petunia × hybrida, blue or purple (8)

WESTERN BUTTERFLY OASIS

Rich in nectar, the plants shown here will attract a variety of butterflies in Zones 8, 9, 12–24. Butterfly bush is, of course, the nonpareil of lures, and as the largest member of the planting it advertises the garden's attractions from afar with its wands of fragrant blue-violet blossoms. But once they arrive, butterflies are likely to linger, moving from one treat to another and yet another.

Bloom is at its most vivid in the first half of summer, but you'll enjoy flowers from midspring until early autumn, long enough to satisfy all the annual butterfly battalions. Sweet alyssum is an annual in all zones, but it produces plenty of volunteer seedlings to carry on from year to year. In Zones 8, 9, 12, and 13, the salvia is also an annual and will need to be replaced each year.

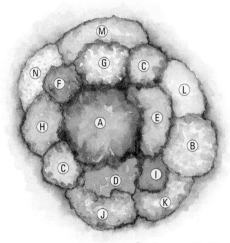

Planting area: 14' x 16'

PLANT LIST

A. **Buddleia davidii 'Empire Blue'.** Butterfly bush (1)

B. **Lantana 'Irene'** (1)

C. **Agapanthus orientalis.** Lily-of-the-Nile (2)

D. **Penstemon × gloxinioides 'Garnet'.** Border penstemon (3)

E. **Centranthus ruber.** Jupiter's beard (4)

F. **Lavandula × intermedia 'Provence'.** Lavandin (1)

G. **Chrysanthemum × superbum 'Alaska'** **(Leucanthemum maximum 'Alaska').** Shasta daisy (6)

H. **Salvia coccinea** (5)

I. **Verbena bonariensis** (1)

J. **Dianthus gratianopolitanus 'Bath's Pink'** **(D. caesius 'Bath's Pink').** Cheddar pink (5)

K. **Scabiosa columbaria.** Pincushion flower (3)

L. **Iberis sempervirens 'Snowflake'.** Evergreen candytuft (2)

M. **Coreopsis grandiflora 'Early Sunrise'** (4)

N. **Lobularia maritima.** Sweet alyssum (5)

BUTTERFLY ISLAND

This could be the perfect butterfly vacation spot: an all-you-can-drink nectar bar. And rising as it does from a sea of lawn, it's both a floral focal point in the landscape and a beacon for butterflies throughout the feeding period. All the plants are suited to Zones 3–9, 14–17, 32–41, regions where, due to the typically long winters, adult butterflies often emerge fairly late in the season. Appropriate to their customers' schedules, these plants begin flowering in late spring (the catmint), then continue through the summer and as far into autumn as climate and the particular year will allow.

PLANT LIST

A. **Vernonia noveboracencis.** Ironweed (3)

B. **Caryopteris × clandonensis.** Blue mist (1)

C. **Spiraea × bumalda 'Anthony Waterer'** (2)

D. **Asclepias tuberosa.** Butterfly weed (3)

E. **Liatris spicata.** Gayfeather (4)

F. **Echinacea purpurea 'Magnus'.** Purple coneflower (5)

G. **Aster × frikartii 'Mönch'** (5)

H. **Agastache foeniculum.** Anise hyssop (1)

I. **Solidago virgaurea 'Goldenmosa'.** Goldenrod (2)

J. **Nepeta × faassenii.** Catmint (5)

K. **Achillea taygetea** (7)

L. **Sedum spectabile 'Meteor' (Hylotelephium spectabile 'Meteor')** (8)

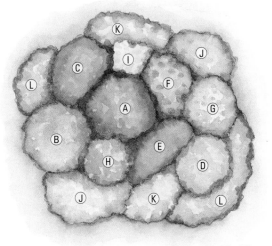

Planting area: 17' x 15'

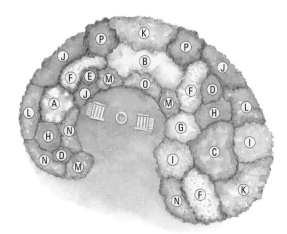

COLOR GARDENS

Hot or cool, loud or muted, flowery or leafy—whatever your preferences in garden color, there's a plan to satisfy you in these pages. The hot-color plantings are bright enough to make you reach for your sunglasses; the white, cool, and gray schemes, in contrast, suggest sweaters and foggy skies. For those who prefer variety to exclusivity, four mixed-color gardens offer inspiration for all climates. And finally—who says foliage alone can't make a colorful planting?

SUMMERTIME BLUES

If a big part of your summer involves trying to escape the heat, this cool collection should bring you at least the illusion of relief. From late spring through a midsummer crescendo until the last aster fades in fall, you'll be soothed by a continuous procession of blossoms in blue, purple, lavender, and white. Anchoring the island garden is a secluded seating area where you can receive your blue therapy at close range. Given regular moisture, all the plants will thrive in Zones 1–7, 32–43. An annual cleanup of the previous year's growth in late winter or early spring will ready the planting for a repeat performance.

PLANT LIST

A. **Paeonia, white cultivar.** Peony (1)

B. **Dictamnus albus 'Albiflorus'.** Gas plant (3)

C. **Baptisia australis.** Blue false indigo (3)

D. **Iris, Siberian, 'Caesar's Brother'** (3)

E. **Allium christophii (A. albopilosum).** Star of Persia (4)

F. **Chrysanthemum × superbum 'Snowbank' or 'Snow Lady' (Leucanthemum maximum 'Snowbank' or 'Snow Lady').** Shasta daisy (14)

G. **Gypsophila paniculata 'Perfecta'.** Baby's breath (1)

H. **Eupatorium coelestinum 'Cori'.** Hardy ageratum (4)

I. **Geranium 'Johnson's Blue'** (2)

J. **Geranium himalayense (G. grandiflorum) 'Birch Double' ('Plenum')** (5)

K. **Nepeta × faassenii.** Catmint (5)

L. **Aster amellus 'Violet Queen'.** Italian aster (7)

M. **Veronica 'Goodness Grows'** (7)

N. **Prunella grandiflora 'Purple Loveliness'.** Self-heal (6)

O. **Dianthus × allwoodii 'Aqua'.** Pink (5)

P. **Hosta 'Francee'** (6)

Planting area: 17' x 15'

SILVER SETTING

Cool, elegant, and restrained, this assemblage of gray, silver, white, ivory, lavender, and pink has an aura of refinement, a sophisticated shimmer that suggests the daytime equivalent of moonlight. Despite the quiet blend of colors, there's no lack of variety here; you'll note a range of plant shapes, leaf sizes, and foliage textures. Iris and allium bloom in spring, but most of the flowering plants put on their show in summer. This patrician pastiche is available to gardeners in much of the country: Zones 2–9, 14–24, 32–41.

Stachys byzantina 'Silver Carpet'

PLANT LIST

A. **Salvia officinalis 'Berggarten'.** Common sage (1)

B. **Malva moschata 'Rosea'.** Musk mallow (2)

C. **Centranthus ruber 'Albus'.** Jupiter's beard (3)

D. **Artemisia absinthium.** Common wormwood (2)

E. **Lysimachia clethroides.** Gooseneck loosestrife (1)

F. **Nepeta × faassenii.** Catmint (3)

G. **Ruta graveolens 'Jackman's Blue'.** Rue (1)

H. **Limonium latifolium.** Sea lavender (3)

I. **Liatris spicata 'Kobold'.** Gayfeather (3)

J. **Verbascum chaixii 'Album'.** Mullein (5)

K. **Helictotrichon sempervirens (Avena sempervirens).** Blue oat grass (2)

L. **Iris, tall bearded, 'Silverado'** (2)

M. **Hemerocallis, cream cultivar.** Daylily (1)

N. **Allium aflatunense** (3)

O. **Achillea clavennae.** Silvery yarrow (7)

P. **Dianthus × allwoodii 'Aqua'.** Pink (6)

Q. **Cerastium tomentosum.** Snow-in-summer (5)

R. **Artemisia stellerana 'Silver Brocade'.** Beach wormwood (3+)

S. **Stachys byzantina 'Silver Carpet'.** Lamb's ears (7)

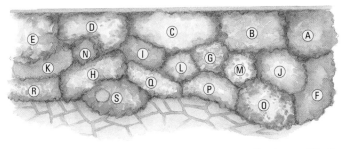

Planting area: 20' x 7'

PLANT LIST

A. **Buddleia davidii 'White Ball'.**
Butterfly bush (1)

B. **Rosa 'Iceberg'** (2)

C. **Euonymus fortunei 'Emerald Gaiety'** (22)

D. **Paeonia, white cultivar.** Peony (2)

E. **Liatris scariosa 'White Spire'.**
Gayfeather (5)

F. **Gypsophila paniculata 'Perfecta'.**
Baby's breath (3)

G. **Chrysanthemum × superbum 'Aglaia'
(Leucanthemum maximum 'Aglaia').**
Shasta daisy (9)

H. **Achillea ptarmica 'The Pearl'** (3)

I. **Centranthus ruber 'Albus'.**
Jupiter's beard (5)

J. **Phlox maculata (P. carolina,
P. suffruticosa) 'Miss Lingard'.**
Thick-leaf phlox (5)

K. **Iris, Siberian, 'Fourfold White'** (3)

L. **Scabiosa caucasica 'Alba'.**
Pincushion flower (3)

M. **Campanula persicifolia, white cultivar.**
Peach-leafed bluebell (4)

N. **Arrhenatherum elatius bulbosum
'Variegatum'.** Bulbous oat grass (4)

O. **Dianthus × allwoodii 'Aqua'.** Pink (4)

P. **Prunella grandiflora 'White Loveliness'.**
Self-heal (7)

Q. **Potentilla alba.** Cinquefoil (5)

PEARLS AND JADE

Plant habits and foliage textures are so varied you may not immediately realize that this plan includes just two colors: white and green. The combination makes for a refreshing, tranquil garden, a perfect spot for taking a breather from the day's activities. Iris, peony, and 'Iceberg' rose bloom in mid- to late spring (depending on zone), with the other plants following close behind; the rose continues right through summer. The plants suggested here all succeed in Zones 3–7, 32–34, 37, and 39. To extend the plan into Zones 35, 36, 38, 40, and 41, use a white cultivar of common lilac (*Syringa vulgaris*) in place of butterfly bush (A in the list at left). In Zones 8, 9, 10, and 14, replace oat grass (N) with lily turf (*Liriope muscari* 'Monroe White'; the lily turf may outperform oat grass in Zones 7, 32, and 33, as well).

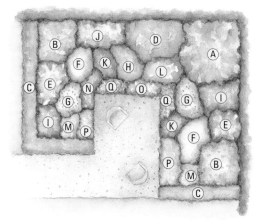

Planting area: 19' x 15'

WHITEWASH

Because many of the plants native to dry-summer, semiarid regions are gray foliaged, a white garden designed for such areas naturally becomes a symphony in white and silver. Carrying the silver banner in this planting are bush morning glory, artemisia, ballota, silvery yarrow, and lamb's ears. Blossoms—all of them in white, of course—begin in midspring with the bearded iris and continue through summer. This scheme flourishes in Zones 8, 9, 14, 18–21; with the simple substitution of *Nerium oleander* 'Morocco' for crape myrtle (A in the plant list), it will also succeed in Zones 15, 16, 22–24.

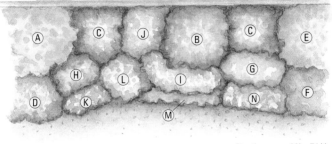

Planting area: 20' x 7½'

PLANT LIST

A. **Lagerstroemia indica 'Petite Snow'.** Crape myrtle (1)

B. **Lantana 'Dwarf White'** (1)

C. **Lavandula × intermedia 'White Spike'.** Lavandin (2)

D. **Convolvulus cneorum.** Bush morning glory (1)

E. **Artemisia arborescens** (1)

F. **Ballota pseudodictamnus** (1)

G. **Agapanthus 'Rancho White' ('Dwarf White', 'Rancho', 'Peter Pan Albus').** Lily-of-the-Nile (4)

H. **Iris, tall bearded, 'Skating Party' or other white cultivar** (3)

I. **Penstemon × gloxinioides 'Holly White'.** Border penstemon (5)

J. **Centranthus ruber 'Albus'.** Jupiter's beard (2)

K. **Gazania, white cultivar** (4)

L. **Achillea clavennae.** Silvery yarrow (4)

M. **Stachys byzantina 'Silver Carpet'.** Lamb's ears (5)

N. **Verbena tenuisecta 'Alba'.** Moss verbena (3)

NORTH STAR

The long, cold winters of higher latitudes and altitudes do limit the variety of plants you can grow, but they put no limits on garden beauty. The planting shown here provides a confettilike cascade of harmonious flower colors from late spring through summer. Foliage is only slightly less varied, featuring leaves in gray as well as green, with an assortment of textures. The 'Jens Munk' rose is heroically hardy, needing just a modicum of cold protection (which can come from snow cover alone, if the winter provides it). The full design is an island, but you can split it into two plans for use against a fence or walk; divide it along the dotted line. The planting is suitable for the coldest zones as well as more temperate regions, succeeding in Zones 1–9, 14–16, 32–45.

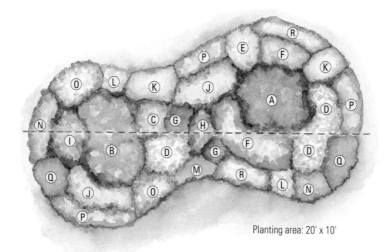

Planting area: 20' x 10'

PLANT LIST

A. Rosa 'Jens Munk' (1)

B. Paeonia, pink cultivar. Peony (2)

C. Campanula persicifolia. Peach-leafed bluebell (2)

D. Gypsophila paniculata 'Perfecta'. Baby's breath (3)

E. Gypsophila paniculata 'Viette's Dwarf' or 'Compacta Plena'. Baby's breath (2)

F. Achillea 'Moonshine' (6)

G. Iris, Siberian, 'Caesar's Brother' (3)

H. Liatris spicata. Gayfeather (3)

I. Liatris spicata 'Kobold'. Gayfeather (4)

J. Hemerocallis 'Happy Returns'. Daylily (7)

K. Oenothera fruticosa (O. tetragona) 'Fireworks' ('Feuerwerkeri', 'Fyrverkeri'). Sundrops (5)

L. Euphorbia epithymoides (E. polychroma) (2)

M. Heuchera × brizoides, pink cultivar. Coral bells (4)

N. Heuchera sanguinea. Coral bells (10)

O. Iberis sempervirens 'Snowflake'. Evergreen candytuft (3)

P. Dianthus × allwoodii, pink cultivar. Pink (12)

Q. Phlox subulata, lavender cultivar. Moss pink (3)

R. Artemisia schmidtiana 'Silver Mound'. Angel's hair (7)

EAST MEETS WEST

Step into this garden, and you could be in Portland or San Jose, Philadelphia or Cleveland. That's the beauty of the plants collected here: adaptability. Their tolerant and flexible nature does not mean they're undistinguished "weeds," though—far from it! From late spring through summer, they provide a knockout, full-palette flower show, given routine watering and little else. As a bonus, a number of the blossoms are good for cutting. Take your ease in this colorful company if you garden in Zones 3–9, 14–21, 32–35, 37, or 39.

PLANT LIST

A. Rosa 'Bonica' (1)

B. Buddleia davidii 'Nanho Purple'. Butterfly bush (1)

C. Panicum virgatum 'Heavy Metal'. Switch grass (1)

D. Nepeta × faassenii 'Six Hills Giant'. Catmint (1)

E. Achillea 'Salmon Beauty'
(A. millefolium 'Salmon Beauty') (2)

F. Achillea 'Moonshine' (3)

G. Chrysanthemum × superbum 'Aglaia'
(Leucanthemum maximum 'Aglaia'). Shasta daisy (7)

H. Penstemon barbatus 'Prairie Fire' (4)

I. Geranium 'Johnson's Blue' (3)

J. Geranium 'Ann Folkard' (2)

K. Coreopsis verticillata 'Zagreb'. Threadleaf coreopsis (1)

L. Scabiosa caucasica. Pincushion flower (3)

M. Hemerocallis 'Stella de Oro'. Daylily (4)

N. Dianthus deltoides 'Zing'. Maiden pink (4)

O. Prunella grandiflora 'Purple Loveliness'. Self-heal (6+)

P. Cerastium tomentosum. Snow-in-summer (7)

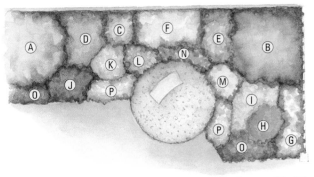

Planting area: 20' x 10'

PLANT LIST

A. Rhaphiolepis (Raphiolepis) 'Majestic Beauty' (multitrunked). India hawthorn (1)

B. Leucophyllum frutescens. Texas ranger (1)

C. Nerium oleander 'Petite Salmon'. Oleander (2)

D. Lavandula × intermedia 'Provence'. Lavandin (2)

E. Salvia leucantha. Mexican sage (2)

F. Gaura lindheimeri (2)

G. Artemisia 'Powis Castle' (2)

H. Penstemon × gloxinioides 'Firebird'. Border penstemon (4)

I. Penstemon × gloxinioides 'Appleblossom'. Border penstemon (4)

J. Agapanthus 'Queen Anne'. Lily-of-the-Nile (4)

K. Dietes vegeta. Fortnight lily (1)

L. Santolina chamaecyparissus. Lavender cotton (1)

M. Convolvulus cneorum. Bush morning glory (1)

N. Convolvulus mauritanicus. Ground morning glory (2)

O. Verbena peruviana (V. chamaedryfolia) (4)

P. Gaillardia × grandiflora 'Goblin Yellow'. Blanket flower (3)

Q. Gazania, mixed colors (8)

R. Cistus 'Victor Reiter'. Rockrose (1)

S. Cistus laurifolius. Rockrose (1)

T. Cistus 'Doris Hibberson'. Rockrose (1)

U. Cistus salviifolius. Sageleaf rockrose (2)

V. Cistus 'Sunset'. Rockrose (2)

W. Cistus 'Warley Rose'. Rockrose (1)

STRICTLY SOUTHWEST

One of the advantages of gardening in Southwestern Zones 12–24 is the mild winter, which favors a great variety of plants. On the down side, though, are the dry conditions that prevail over much of the territory for much of the year. Except for a few desert areas where showers come in summer, winter is the rainy season—and that means that you, not nature, will be providing the garden with water from spring through summer and into autumn. No wonder, then, that plantings thriving on just moderate moisture are highly favored in these zones. When you choose the plan shown here, you can trade hauling the hose for reclining on the chaise to soak up some sun. The most concentrated color display runs from midspring into the first half of summer, though in milder-summer regions the show will continue unabated until early autumn, when vibrant purple Mexican sage provides the garden's grand finale.

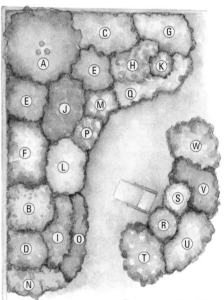

Planting area: 20' x 15'

BI-COASTAL TROPICS

You're not in Kansas anymore. This is Honolulu…or Miami…or San Diego, where frost is a stranger and tropical luxuriance is the norm. The plant assortment shown here, while tender, is still tough enough to weather the occasional slight frost, making it suitable not only to Zone 25 but also to Zones 24, 26, and 27. Prominent are several signature plants of tropic climes: kahili ginger, colorful Chinese hibiscus, and that epitome of jungle foliage, elephant's ear. When bloom is at its peak in summer, you'll also be treated to intoxicating fragrances from the angel's trumpet, ginger, and gardenia. Most of these plants are permanent shrubs and perennials; the coleus, New Guinea hybrid impatiens, and star clusters may live into a second year, but the display is usually better if plants are replaced annually.

Planting area: 20' x 16'

PLANT LIST

A. Brugmansia candida. Angel's trumpet (1)

B. Tibouchina urvilleana. Princess flower (1)

C. Hibiscus rosa-sinensis 'Fiesta' or 'Ross Estey'. Chinese hibiscus (1)

D. Mandevilla 'Alice du Pont' (1)

E. Brunfelsia pauciflora 'Macrantha'. Yesterday-today-and-tomorrow (1)

F. Justicia brandegeana (Beloperone guttata). Shrimp plant (2)

G. Cuphea ignea. Cigar plant (5)

H. Phygelius × rectus 'African Queen'. Cape fuchsia (2)

I. Hemerocallis (evergreen), yellow cultivar. Daylily (6+)

J. Liriope muscari 'Silvery Sunproof'. Big blue lily turf (14)

K. Clivia miniata. Kaffir lily (9)

L. Zantedeschia aethiopica. Common calla (2)

M. Colocasia esculenta 'Black Magic'. Elephant's ear, taro (2)

N. Hedychium gardneranum. Kahili ginger (3)

O. Chlorophytum comosum 'Variegatum' or 'Vittatum'. Spider plant (12)

P. Pentas lanceolata. Star clusters (4)

Q. Impatiens, New Guinea hybrid, 'Tango' (3)

R. Zoysia tenuifolia. Korean grass (sprigs or plugs, set 6 inches apart)

S. Gardenia jasminoides 'White Gem' (1)

T. Caladium bicolor 'White Queen'. Fancy-leafed caladium (3)

U. Coleus × hybridus (3)

TROPIC TEMPO

Neon-brilliant reds, oranges, and yellows are tempered with splashes of dark blue and purple in a tropical tapestry so vivid it virtually vibrates. Even the dominant foliage plants—canna and New Zealand flax—carry out the bright, hot theme. The planting is long and fairly narrow, suitable for a spot at the front of a garden or along a walkway, where it's certain to grab any passerby's attention. At its blazing best from late spring through summer, this assortment thrives in Zones 14–24.

PLANT LIST

A. **Phormium 'Maori Chief'.**
New Zealand flax (1)

B. **Rosa 'Charisma'** (1)

C. **Canna 'Phasion' ('Tropicanna')**
or 'Pretoria' (3)

D. **Felicia amelloides 'San Gabriel'**
or 'San Luis'. Blue marguerite (1)

E. **Penstemon × gloxinioides 'Firebird'.**
Border penstemon (3)

F. **Ratibida columnifera.** Mexican hat (4)

G. **Hemerocallis, red cultivar.** Daylily (3)

H. **Hemerocallis, orange cultivar.** Daylily (4)

I. **Hemerocallis 'Stella de Oro'.** Daylily (3)

J. **Agapanthus 'Storm Cloud'.**
Lily-of-the-Nile (2)

K. **Coreopsis grandiflora 'Early Sunrise'** (7)

L. **Coreopsis verticillata 'Zagreb'.**
Threadleaf coreopsis (2)

M. **Gaillardia × grandiflora 'Goblin'.**
Blanket flower (7)

N. **Osteospermum fruticosum 'African Queen'**
or 'Burgundy'. Trailing African daisy (3)

O. **Verbena tenuisecta 'Tapien Purple'.**
Moss verbena (8)

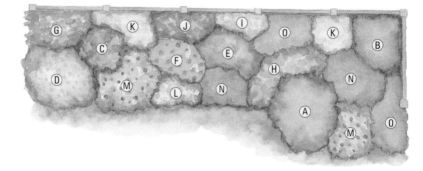

Planting area: 20' x 7'

HEAT WAVE

Unabashedly hot, this lava-bright combination of perennials and two annuals puts on a summer-long show in Zones 1–9, 14–21, 31–43. The dominant plant is the annual Mexican sunflower, which zooms up and out like Jack's beanstalk, quickly reaching shrublike proportions. The other annual is that old favorite, French marigold—much lower than the sunflower, but almost as striking when massed in a tight circle to form a pool of glowing color. You can use this design as an island; it's especially stunning when set in a green lawn. Or modify it to form a curving bed along a fence: divide it along the dotted line, then plant the larger half.

PLANT LIST

A. Rudbeckia fulgida sullivantii 'Goldsturm'.
   Black-eyed Susan (3)

B. Achillea 'Fireland' (2)

C. Achillea 'Moonshine' (7)

D. Asclepias tuberosa, Gay Butterflies strain. Butterfly weed (3)

E. Hemerocallis, orange cultivar. Daylily (3)

F. Hemerocallis, cream or light yellow cultivar. Daylily (2)

G. Hemerocallis 'Black-eyed Stella'. Daylily (3)

H. Oenothera fruticosa (O. tetragona) 'Fireworks'
   ('Feuerwerkeri', 'Fyrverkeri'). Sundrops (2)

I. Gaillardia × grandiflora 'Tokajer'. Blanket flower (4)

J. Coreopsis auriculata 'Nana' (4)

K. Potentilla atrosanguinea 'Gibson's Scarlet'. Cinquefoil (6)

L. Tithonia rotundifolia (T. speciosa). Mexican sunflower (5)

M. Tagetes patula. French marigold (10)

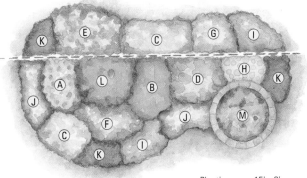

Planting area: 15' x 8'

Berberis thunbergii 'Aurea'

WHO NEEDS FLOWERS?

When foliage forms a vivid patchwork like this, flowers are irrelevant! From the start of the growing season until leaf-fall in autumn, the planting is consistently colorful, presenting a striking combination of wine red, glowing yellow, chartreuse, steely blue, silver gray, and green-and-cream (in the variegated foliage of cotoneaster and eulalia grass). Dominating the plan is a golden privet that's almost too bright to believe; its vivid hue is repeated more subtly in the 'Aurea' barberry and the spiraea, forming a yellow thread that weaves throughout the foliage tapestry. All the plants are tough customers, suited to a sunny site in Zones 2–11, 14–21, 32–41.

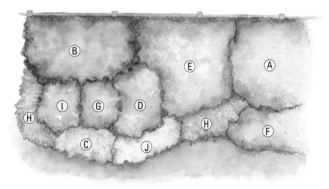

Planting area: 28' x 13'

PLANT LIST

A. **Ligustrum × vicaryi**. Vicary golden privet (1)

B. **Berberis thunbergii 'Atropurpurea'.** Red-leaf Japanese barberry (2)

C. **Berberis thunbergii 'Aurea'.** Japanese barberry (2)

D. **Spiraea × bumalda 'Goldflame'** (2)

E. **Cotoneaster horizontalis 'Variegata'.** Rock cotoneaster (3)

F. **Juniperus sabina 'Blue Danube'.** Savin juniper (4+)

G. **Miscanthus sinensis 'Morning Light'.** Eulalia grass (1)

H. **Festuca 'Elijah Blue'.** Blue fescue (10)

I. **Salvia officinalis 'Berggarten'.** Common sage (1)

J. **Artemisia stellerana 'Silver Brocade'.** Beach wormwood (4)

SAY IT WITH FOLIAGE

If the plan on the facing page is a bold quilt, this one is more like a needlepoint design, featuring more variety and a greater number of plants. The red-leafed Japanese maple sets the lightly shaded scene, where a host of shrubs and perennials sparkle in yellow, blue, silver, burgundy, and white-and-green. The focus is on foliage: the flowers of the lady's-mantle are subtle, while those of the hostas are so fleeting as to be immaterial. Only the daphne has conspicuous blossoms—but you'll forgive their showiness when you breathe in their heady scent. This grouping grows best where there's a bit of atmospheric moisture: Zones 3–6, 14–17, 32, 34, 35, 37, 39. Gardeners in Zones 33, 36, 40, and 41 can use the plan as well by replacing the holly (C in the list below) with *Euonymus fortunei* 'Canadale Gold'.

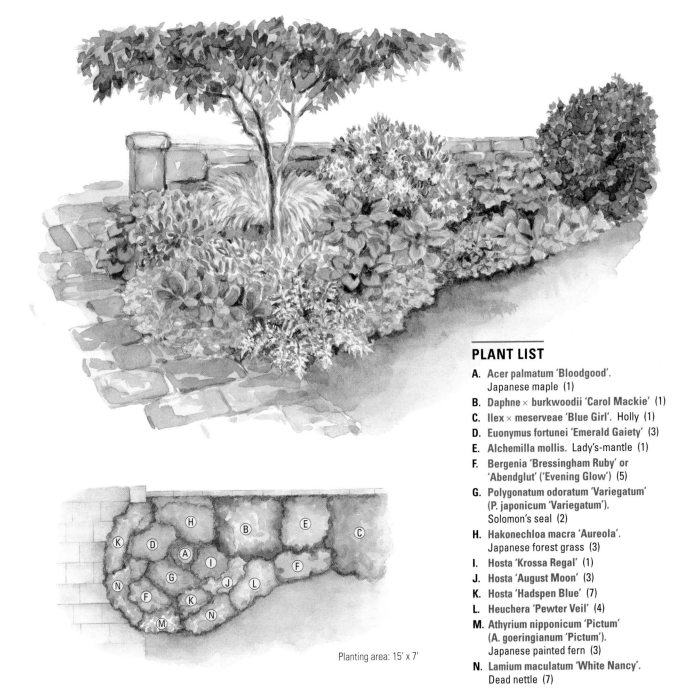

Planting area: 15' x 7'

PLANT LIST

A. Acer palmatum 'Bloodgood'. Japanese maple (1)

B. Daphne × burkwoodii 'Carol Mackie' (1)

C. Ilex × meserveae 'Blue Girl'. Holly (1)

D. Euonymus fortunei 'Emerald Gaiety' (3)

E. Alchemilla mollis. Lady's-mantle (1)

F. Bergenia 'Bressingham Ruby' or 'Abendglut' ('Evening Glow') (5)

G. Polygonatum odoratum 'Variegatum' (P. japonicum 'Variegatum'). Solomon's seal (2)

H. Hakonechloa macra 'Aureola'. Japanese forest grass (3)

I. Hosta 'Krossa Regal' (1)

J. Hosta 'August Moon' (3)

K. Hosta 'Hadspen Blue' (7)

L. Heuchera 'Pewter Veil' (4)

M. Athyrium nipponicum 'Pictum' (A. goeringianum 'Pictum'). Japanese painted fern (3)

N. Lamium maculatum 'White Nancy'. Dead nettle (7)

SUNSET'S GARDEN CLIMATE ZONES

A plant's performance is governed by the total climate: length of growing season, timing and amount of rainfall, winter lows, summer highs, humidity. *Sunset*'s climate zone maps take all these factors into account—unlike the familiar hardiness zone maps devised by the U.S. Department of Agriculture, which divide the U.S. and Canada into zones based strictly on winter lows. The U.S.D.A. maps tell you only where a plant may survive the winter; our climate zone maps let you see where that plant will thrive year-round. Below are brief descriptions of the 45 zones illustrated on the map on pages 108–109. For more information, consult *Sunset*'s *National Garden Book* and *Western Garden Book*.

ZONE 1. Coldest Winters in the West and Western Prairie States

Growing season: early June through Aug., but with some variation—the longest seasons are usually found near this zone's large bodies of water. Frost can come any night of the year. Winters are snowy and intensely cold, due to latitude, elevation, and/or influence of continental air mass. There's some summer rainfall.

ZONE 2. Second-coldest Western Climate

Growing season: early May through Sept. Winters are cold (lows run from −3° to −34°F/−19° to −37°C), but less so than in Zone 1. In northern and interior areas, lower elevations fall into Zone 2, higher areas into Zone 1.

ZONE 3. West's Mildest High-elevation and Interior Regions

Growing season: early May to late Sept.—shorter than in Zone 2, but offset by milder winters (lows from 13° to −24°F/−11° to −31°C). This is fine territory for plants needing winter chill and dry, hot summers.

ZONE 4. Cold-winter Western Washington and British Columbia

Growing season: early May to early Oct. Summers are cool, thanks to ocean influence; chilly winters (19° to −7°F/−7° to −22°C) result from elevation, influence of continental air mass, or both. Coolness, ample rain suit many perennials and bulbs.

ZONE 5. Ocean-influenced Northwest Coast and Puget Sound

Growing season: mid-April to Nov., typically with cool temperatures throughout. Less rain falls here than in Zone 4; winter lows range from 28° to 1°F/−2° to −17°C. This "English garden" climate is ideal for rhododendrons and many rock garden plants.

ZONE 6. Oregon's Willamette Valley

Growing season: mid-Mar. to mid-Nov., with somewhat warmer temperatures than in Zone 5. Ocean influence keeps winter lows about the same as in Zone 5. Climate suits all but tender plants and those needing hot or dry summers.

ZONE 7. Oregon's Rogue River Valley, California's High Foothills

Growing season: May to early Oct. Summers are hot and dry; typical winter lows run from 23° to 9°F/−5° to −13°C. The summer-winter contrast suits plants that need dry, hot summers and moist, only moderately cold winters.

ZONE 8. Cold-air Basins of California's Central Valley

Growing season: mid-Feb. through Nov. This is a valley floor with no maritime influence. Summers are hot; winter lows range from 29° to 13°F/−2° to −11°C. Rain comes in the cooler months, covering just the early part of the growing season.

ZONE 9. Thermal Belts of California's Central Valley

Growing season: late Feb. through Dec. Zone 9 is located in the higher elevations around Zone 8, but its summers are just as hot; its winter lows are slightly higher (temperatures range from 28° to 18°F/−2° to −8°C). Rainfall pattern is the same as in Zone 8.

ZONE 10. High Desert Areas of Arizona, New Mexico, West Texas, Oklahoma Panhandle, and Southwest Kansas

Growing season: April to early Nov. Chilly (even snow-dusted) weather rules from late Nov. through Feb., with lows from 31° to 24°F/−1° to −4°C. Rain comes in summer as well as in the cooler seasons.

ZONE 11. Medium to High Desert of California and Southern Nevada

Growing season: early April to late Oct. Summers are sizzling, with 110 days above 90°F/32°C. Balancing this is a 3½-month winter, with 85 nights below freezing and lows from 11° to 0°F/−12° to −18°C. Scant rainfall comes in winter.

ZONE 12. Arizona's Intermediate Desert

Growing season: mid-Mar. to late Nov., with scorching midsummer heat. Compared to Zone 13, this region has harder frosts; record low is 6°F/−14°C. Rains come in summer and winter.

ZONE 13. Low or Subtropical Desert

Growing season: mid-Feb. through Nov., interrupted by nearly 3 months of incandescent, growth-stopping summer heat. Most frosts are light (record lows run from 19° to 13°F/−17° to −11°C); scant rain comes in summer and winter.

ZONE 14. Inland Northern and Central California with Some Ocean Influence

Growing season: early Mar. to mid-Nov., with rain coming in the remaining months. Periodic intrusions of marine air temper summer heat and winter cold (lows run from 26° to 16°F/−3° to −9°C). Mediterranean-climate plants are at home here.

ZONE 15. Northern and Central California's Chilly-winter Coast-influenced Areas

Growing season: Mar. to Dec. Rain comes from fall through winter. Typical winter lows range from 28° to 21°F/−2° to −6°C. Maritime air influences the zone much of the time, giving it cooler, moister summers than Zone 14.

ZONE 16. Northern and Central California Coast Range Thermal Belts

Growing season: late Feb. to late Nov. With cold air draining to lower elevations, winter lows typically run from 32° to 19°F/0° to −7°C. Like Zone 15, this region is dominated by maritime air, but its winters are milder on average.

ZONE 17. Oceanside Northern and Central California and Southernmost Oregon

Growing season: late Feb. to early Dec. Coolness and fog are hallmarks; summer highs seldom top 75°F/24°C, while winter lows run from 36° to 23°F/2° to −5°C. Heat-loving plants disappoint or dwindle here.

ZONE 18. Hilltops and Valley Floors of Interior Southern California

Growing season: mid-Mar. through late Nov. Summers are hot and dry; rain comes in winter, when lows reach 28° to 10°F/−2° to −12°C. Plants from the Mediterranean and Near Eastern regions thrive here.

ZONE 19. Thermal belts around Southern California's Interior Valleys

Growing season: early Mar. through Nov. As in Zone 18, rainy winters and hot, dry summers are the norm—but here, winter lows dip only to 27° to 22°F/−3° to −6°C, allowing some tender evergreen plants to grow outdoors with protection.

ZONE 20. Hilltops and Valley Floors of Ocean-influenced Inland Southern California

Growing season: late Mar. to late Nov.—but fairly mild winters (lows of 28° to 23°F/−2° to −5°C) allow gardening through much of the year. Cool and moist maritime influence alternates with hot, dry interior air.

ZONE 21. Thermal Belts around Southern California's Ocean-influenced Interior Valleys

Growing season: early Mar. to early Dec., with the same tradeoff of oceanic and interior influence as in Zone 20. During the winter rainy season, lows range from 36° to 23°F/2° to −5°C—warmer than in Zone 20, since the colder air drains to the valleys.

ZONE 22. Colder-winter Parts of Southern California's Coastal Region

Growing season: Mar. to early Dec. Winter lows seldom fall below 28°F/–2°C (records are around 21°F/–6°C), though colder air sinks to this zone from Zone 23. Summers are warm; rain comes in winter. Climate here is largely oceanic.

ZONE 23. Thermal Belts of Southern California's Coastal Region

Growing season: almost year-round (all but first half of Jan.). Rain comes in winter. Reliable ocean influence keeps summers mild (except when hot Santa Ana winds come from inland), frosts negligible; 23°F/–5°C is the record low.

ZONE 24. Marine-dominated Southern California Coast

Growing season: all year, but periodic freezes have dramatic effects (record lows are 33° to 20°F/1° to –7°C). Climate here is oceanic (but warmer than oceanic Zone 17), with cool summers, mild winters. Subtropical plants thrive.

ZONE 25. South Florida and the Keys

Growing season: all year. Add ample year-round rainfall (least in Dec. through Mar.), high humidity, and overall warmth, and you have a near-tropical climate. The Keys are frost-free; winter lows elsewhere run from 40° to 25°F/4° to –4°C.

ZONE 26. Central and Interior Florida

Growing season: early Feb. to late Dec., with typically humid, warm to hot weather. Rain is plentiful all year, heaviest in summer and early fall. Lows range from 15°F/–9°C in the north to 27°F/–3°C in the south; arctic air brings periodic hard freezes.

ZONE 27. Lower Rio Grande Valley

Growing season: early Mar. to mid-Dec.. Summers are hot and humid; winter lows only rarely dip below freezing. Many plants from tropical and subtropical Africa and South America are well adapted here.

ZONE 28. Gulf Coast, North Florida, Atlantic Coast to Charleston

Growing season: mid-Mar. to early Dec. Humidity and rainfall are year-round phenomena; summers are hot, winters virtually frostless but subject to periodic invasions by frigid arctic air. Azaleas, camellias, many subtropicals flourish.

ZONE 29. Interior Plains of South Texas

Growing season: mid-Mar. through Nov. Moderate rainfall (to 25" annually) comes year-round. Summers are hot. Winter lows can dip to 26°F/–3°C, with occasional arctic freezes bringing much lower readings.

ZONE 30. Hill Country of Central Texas

Growing season: mid-Mar. through Nov. Zone 30 has higher annual rainfall than Zone 29 (to 35") and lower winter temperatures, normally to around 20°F/–7°C. Seasonal variations favor many fruit crops, perennials.

ZONE 31. Interior Plains of Gulf Coast and Coastal Southeast

Growing season: mid-Mar. to early Nov. In this extensive east-west zone, hot and sticky summers contrast with chilly winters (record low temperatures are 7° to 0°F/–14° to –18°C). There's rain all year (an annual average of 50"), with the least falling in Oct.

ZONE 32. Interior Plains of Mid-Atlantic States; Chesapeake Bay, Southeastern Pennsylvania, Southern New Jersey

Growing season: late Mar. to early Nov. Rain falls year-round (40" to 50" annually); winter lows (moving through the zone from south to north) are 30° to 20°F/–1° to –7°C. Humidity is less oppressive here than in Zone 31.

ZONE 33. North-Central Texas and Oklahoma Eastward to the Appalachian Foothills

Growing season: mid-April through Oct. Warm Gulf Coast air and colder continental/arctic fronts both play a role; their unpredictable interplay results in a wide range in annual rainfall (22" to 52") and winter lows (20° to 0°F/–7° to –18°C). Summers are muggy and warm to hot.

ZONE 34. Lowlands and Coast from Gettysburg to North of Boston

Growing season: late April to late Oct. Ample rainfall and humid summers are the norm. Winters are variable—typically fairly mild (around 20°F/–7°C), but with lows down to –3° to –22°F/–19° to –30°C if arctic air swoops in.

ZONE 35. Ouachita Mountains, Northern Oklahoma and Arkansas, Southern Kansas to North-Central Kentucky and Southern Ohio

Growing season: late April to late Oct. Rain comes in all seasons. Summers can be truly hot and humid. Without arctic fronts, winter lows are around 18°F/–8°C; with them, the coldest weather may bring lows of –20°F/–29°C.

ZONE 36. Appalachian Mountains

Growing season: May to late Oct. Thanks to greater elevation, summers are cooler and less humid, winters colder (0° to –20°F/–18° to –29°C) than in adjacent, lower zones. Rain comes all year (heaviest in spring). Late frosts are common.

ZONE 37. Hudson Valley and Appalachian Plateau

Growing season: May to mid-Oct., with rainfall throughout. Lower in elevation than neighboring Zone 42, with warmer winters: lows are 0° to –5°F/–18° to –21°C, unless arctic air moves in. Summer is warm to hot, humid.

ZONE 38. New England Interior and Lowland Maine

Growing season: May to early Oct. Summers feature reliable rainfall and lack oppressive humidity of lower-elevation, more southerly areas. Winter lows dip to –10° to –20°F/–23° to –29°C, with periodic colder temperatures due to influxes of arctic air.

ZONE 39. Shoreline Regions of the Great Lakes

Growing season: early May to early Oct. Springs and summers are cooler here, autumns milder than in areas farther from the lakes. Southeast lakeshores get the heaviest snowfalls. Lows reach 0° to –10°F/–18° to –23°C.

ZONE 40. Inland Plains of Lake Erie and Lake Ontario

Growing season: mid-May to mid-Sept., with rainy, warm, variably humid weather. The lakes help moderate winter lows; temperatures typically range from –10° to –20°F/–23° to –29°C, with occasional colder readings when arctic fronts rush through.

ZONE 41. Northeast Kansas and Southeast Nebraska to Northern Illinois and Indiana, Southeast Wisconsin, Michigan, Northern Ohio

Growing season: early May to early Oct. Winter brings average lows of –11° to –20°F/–23° to –29°C. Summers in this zone are hotter and longer west of the Mississippi, cooler and shorter nearer the Great Lakes; summer rainfall increases in the same west-to-east direction.

ZONE 42. Interior Pennsylvania and New York; St. Lawrence Valley

Growing season: late May to late Sept. This zone's elevation gives it colder winters than surrounding zones: lows range from –20° to –40°F/–29° to –40°C, with the colder readings coming in the Canadian portion of the zone. Summers are humid, rainy.

ZONE 43. Upper Mississippi Valley, Upper Michigan, Southern Ontario and Quebec

Growing season: late May to mid-Sept. The climate is humid from spring through early fall; summer rains are usually dependable. Arctic air dominates in winter, with lows typically from –20° to –30°F/–29° to –34°C.

ZONE 44. Mountains of New England and Southeastern Quebec

Growing season: June to mid-Sept. Latitude and elevation give fairly cool, rainy summers, cold winters with lows of –20° to –40°F/–29° to –40°C. Choose short-season, low heat-requirement annuals and vegetables.

ZONE 45. Northern Parts of Minnesota and Wisconsin, Eastern Manitoba through Interior Quebec

Growing season: mid-June through Aug., with rain throughout; rainfall (and humidity) are least in zone's western part, greatest in eastern reaches. Winters are frigid (–30° to –40°F/–34° to –40°C), with snow cover, deeply frozen soil.

Sunset's Garden Climate Zones

Climate Zones | 1 2 3 4 5 6 7 8 9 10 11 12 13 14 15 16 17 18 19 20 21 22

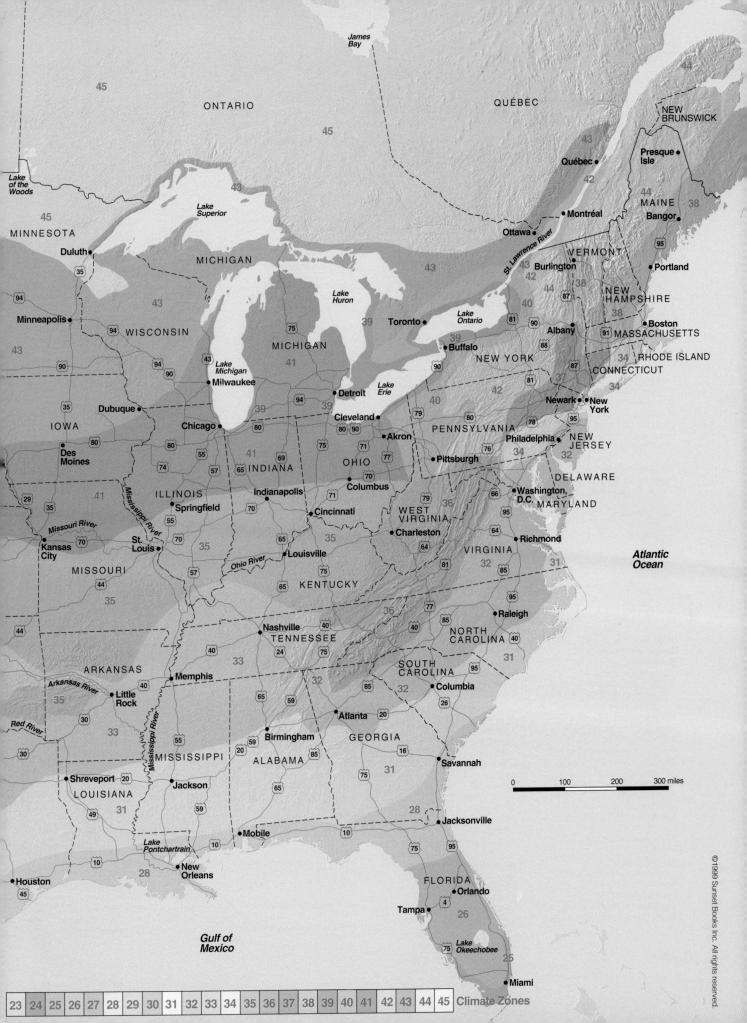

| 23 | 24 | 25 | 26 | 27 | 28 | 29 | 30 | 31 | 32 | 33 | 34 | 35 | 36 | 37 | 38 | 39 | 40 | 41 | 42 | 43 | 44 | 45 | Climate Zones |

SUBJECT INDEX

PLANT INDEX